Radiosondes, carried aloft by balloons, transmit reports on conditions in the upper air to a receiving unit on the survey ship. The reports include data on temperature, air pressure and humidity.

Scientific facts are collected by instruments towed by survey ships. Only when a ship is moving at a slow speed can nets be towed to collect samples of the minute organisms in the water. A "sparker" fastened to a long cable transmits low frequency sound signals that penetrate the sea bottom. The echoes of the signals tell the character of the rock formation and sediment.

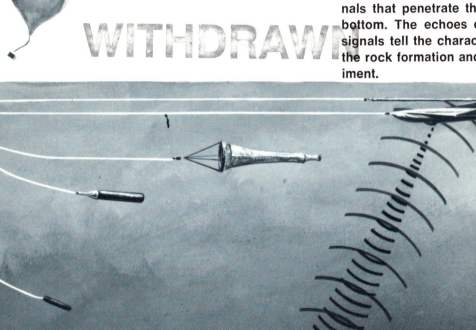

Charting the Oceans

Other books by
RUTH BRINDZE
published by The Vanguard Press

THE GULF STREAM
THE STORY OF OUR CALENDAR
THE STORY OF THE TOTEM POLE
THE STORY OF GOLD
THE STORY OF THE TRADE WINDS

Charting

the Oceans

by Ruth Brindze

The Vanguard Press, Inc., New York

International Standard Book Number: 0-8149-0715-6
Library of Congress Catalog Card Number: 77-134674

Table of Contents

List of Illustrations

Charting the Oceans

*There are no marked highways on the water and there is no one
of whom inquiries can be made.*

Millions of Miles
Without Roads

Almost everyone who makes a trip by car uses road maps. Yet one can get along without them because directional signs are posted along highways and advice about routes can be obtained by stopping and making inquiries.

The conditions with which the navigator of a boat must cope are altogether different. There are no marked highways on the water and there is no one of whom inquiries can be made. Whether a navigator is to make a trip of 25 miles or of 2500 miles, he must plot his own route. To do this he needs maps.

With a sea map (usually called a chart) a navigator can determine the direction he must steer, the number of miles he must cover to reach his destination, and the depth of the water. His chart tells him where he must detour to avoid danger areas, the shape of coastlines, the location of light-houses and other prominent structures that can be used as guides, and many other facts important to navigators of big boats and small ones.

Chart-making began when men started to travel by boat. Ancient explorers who paddled, rowed, and sailed along the

shore made rough sketches of it to use on subsequent trips. As men dared to sail farther and farther, their mapping and records became more elaborate. Seafarers recorded the courses to steer from one place to another, the location of well-sheltered harbors, of streams from which they had replenished their supply of drinking water, and other useful information. We know about these ancient guides because a few have been found. One, written more than two thousand years ago by a man named Pytheas, describes his voyage from Greece to Scotland, Norway, and Germany.

For a long time charting was done by explorers. Now it is done by specialists, and the production of charts has become a vast and continuous scientific undertaking. Charting the oceans is one of the biggest and most challenging mapping projects on our planet. Its primary purpose today, as in the past, is to provide seafarers with the information required for safe navigation. But all of us stand to gain from the charting of the seas, for it provides a view of inner space—the hidden, and mysterious underwater world.

This portrait of Christopher Columbus hangs in the Royal Gallery at Naples, Italy. It shows the explorer as he looked when he was a favorite at the royal court.

CHAPTER I

State Secrets

When Christopher Columbus returned to Spain after his first voyage to America, the only things he brought back that were considered to be of real value were the maps he had drawn of his ocean route and of the land he had discovered. King Ferdinand and Queen Isabella, who had financed the expedition, expected to be repaid with vast quantities of gold, silver, pearls, and spices. Although the voyage had not produced the anticipated riches, Spain's rulers believed Columbus had reached his goal, India, and that other voyages there would produce fabulous treasures. For this reason, Columbus's maps were guarded as state secrets. Maps and records of the explorer's three later voyages also were kept secret.

An elaborate plan was developed by the Spanish government to regulate travel to "las Indias," the name then used for America. The government's control system was based on the secret maps. Copies of these sea charts could be obtained only by captains officially authorized to sail to "las Indias."

Sea charts had been treated as secret documents before the reign of Ferdinand and Isabella, for if a captain has a chart he can find his way to any place on it. Therefore, just

as pirates hid their sketches of the spot where they had buried loot to prevent others from stealing it, so nations attempted to protect their rights to territories that they knew, or thought, were sources of riches by keeping the charts to such places secret.

Ferdinand and Isabella introduced a new idea in ocean charting. They established a department to prepare and issue charts. Each captain who was granted a license to sail to "las Indias" was ordered to map "every land, bay, harbor and other things new and worthy of being noted." When a captain returned to Spain he was obligated to give his sketches and notes to the chief of the government's map department, an official known as the Pilot Major. The Pilot Major was responsible for making additions and corrections to the government's master set of charts.

But few captains, and especially not those who expected to sail again to Spain's new territories, gave the Pilot Major a full report of what they had learned. Some reported little or nothing about the best routes, the best harbors, and so on. Captains who had such information saw no reason to divulge it. They did not want to reveal what might help competitors.

Not only was information withheld, but there was no way for the Pilot Major to check the facts he was given. If Captain A gave one location for a place and Captain B another, the Pilot Major could only guess which of the two was correct. The result was that the official charts were no more accurate than those sold at lower prices by private map makers who knew many seafarers and paid them well for information. Map makers also copied from one another. There were private map makers in every large seaport from whom captains, whether licensed or unlicensed, could obtain charts.

Before his voyages of discovery, Columbus had worked

for many years as a map maker. Unfortunately, only one of the charts he made during his voyages has been preserved. That one, of the northern coast of Haiti, is proof of the explorer's skill in mapping. Although Columbus's sketch includes no details, it portrays the coast almost exactly as it is shown on modern charts.

Captains of Spanish ships were subject to heavy fines for sailing to America without the government's authorization and the purchase of official charts, but it was comparatively easy to evade the government's regulations by using small ports where no inspectors were stationed to check on the departure or arrival of ships. Nor could Spain prevent ships of other nations from crossing the Atlantic.

Yet Spain's idea of issuing official maps of the sea set an important precedent. Today every maritime nation publishes charts. Anyone can buy them; prices are low.

Some information for charts is still supplied by seafarers, but most of it is collected by government-employed experts. The United States divides responsibility for ocean charting between the National Ocean Survey, which prepares and publishes charts of the nation's coastal waters, and the Naval Oceanographic Office (a branch of the U. S. Navy), which issues charts for other parts of the world.

No country works alone in charting the seas. Nations exchange data. Thus, charts of the French coast published by the United States for use by American navigators are based largely on measurements made by French surveyors, and charts of the American coast published by other nations are based largely on measurements made by the men of the National Ocean Survey. The International Hydrographic Bureau, founded in 1919 for pooling and increasing navigational knowledge, has functioned most successfully. (Hydrography is the science of measuring and mapping bodies of water.)

Yet, despite the co-operation among nations, the job of charting the oceans is not nearly completed. Even along the coasts of the United States there are areas that have not yet been fully mapped.

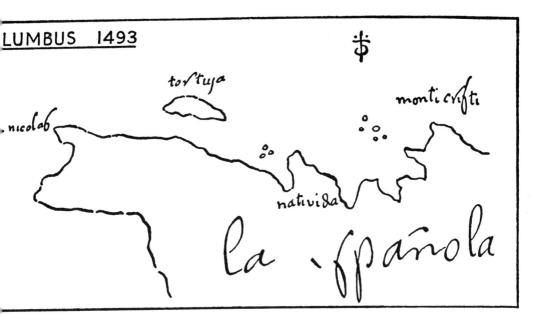

LUMBUS 1493

tortuja

monti crifti

nicolaб

nativida

la ʃpañola

*Of all the charts drawn by Columbus, only this one of the north-
ern coast of Haiti has been preserved. It was made during the
explorer's first voyage to America.*

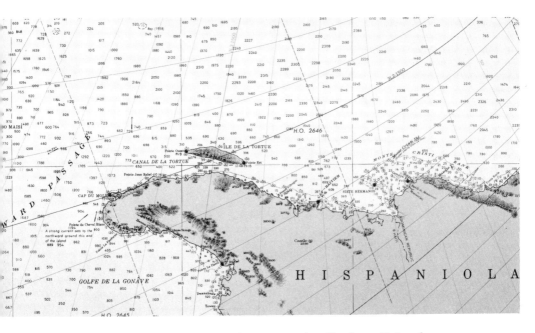

*A modern chart of Haiti supplies more details than Columbus
included but shows the coast almost exactly as the explorer
sketched it.*

CHAPTER II

The World's Biggest

Mapping Job

The oceans cover more than 70 per cent of the surface of our planet, and the world's coasts, the boundaries between land and sea, are millions of miles in length. The shoreline of the United States (including Hawaii and Alaska) extends for nearly 90,000 miles.

Even if it were necessary to make only measurements of the surface of the oceans, the task would be immense. But to produce a useful chart the depth of the water also must be measured.

Depth figures are especially important to navigators when operating in coastal areas. Fewer ships sink in the deep water of mid-ocean than are wrecked near the shore, where there are many natural hazards. Rocks, sand, and mud bars, hidden by a shallow layer of water, can be safely by-passed only if their location is accurately shown on charts.

Surveyors collecting the data for a chart cannot see, any more than can the navigator of a boat, where the water is deep and where it is shallow. Until comparatively recently surveyors measured the depth of water by lowering a heavy

Whether waves are breaking, or the sea is calm, navigators depend on charts to plot a safe course to their destination.

lead weight to the sea bottom. How many feet of rope or wire reeled out until the lead touched the bottom told the depth. A measurement of the depth of water beneath a boat is known as a "sounding."

Lowering and pulling up a lead weight took so much time that only a limited number of soundings could be made when an area was surveyed. The result was that many danger spots were not discovered until boats were wrecked on them. Now surveyors use electronic instruments to record the depth of the water along the entire path the surveying boat travels.

These electronic instruments, called echo sounders, beam

a sound signal to the bottom, time the interval until the signal is echoed back, and convert the time interval into the distance to the bottom. Some echo sounders merely flash the depth figure on a dial; other echo sounders make a continuous drawing showing the water's depth; and still others record their measurements on a tape that is fed into a computer for analysis. Survey ships are often equipped with instruments capable of recording depth measurements by all three methods.

Until the development of echo sounders, few probes were made in mid-ocean because of the time required and the difficulty of lowering a lead weight through miles of water. Now that soundings are made electronically, we are getting a picture of the mountains, canyons, and plains in the deepest parts of the underwater world that no man may ever see.

Echo sounder on board a survey vessel drawing a graph of ocean bottom. This precision instrument can probe depths of more than half a mile.

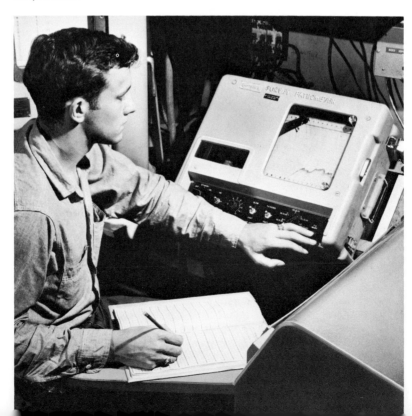

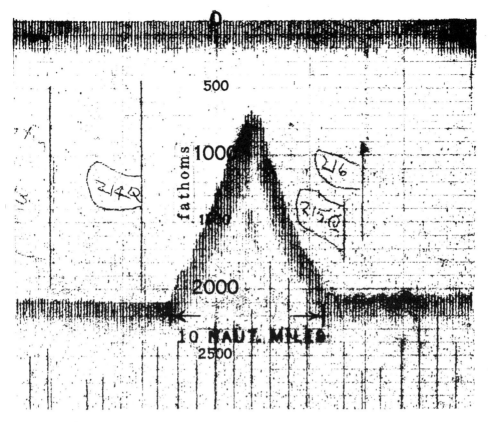

Graph of an underwater volcanic seamount nearly a mile and a half high, the base of which extends for more than ten miles.

Echo sounders tell where there are mountains by recording a decrease in the depth of the water. As a ship passes over the side of a submerged mountain, the water becomes progressively shallower. The water is shallowest at the mountain's peak.

Canyons are located by a sharp increase in the depth of the water recorded by an echo sounder. Not long ago the echo sounders on a survey ship working in the Pacific Ocean recorded such an increase. The surveyors realized they were over a previously unknown canyon. To explore it, the ship crisscrossed the area many times while its echo sounders traced the boundaries of the deeper water. The measurements indicated that the canyon was about 800 miles long and 15 miles wide. Compared to this canyon,

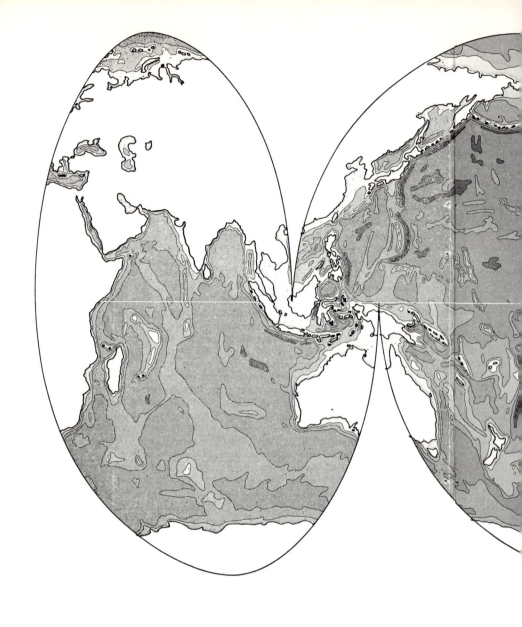

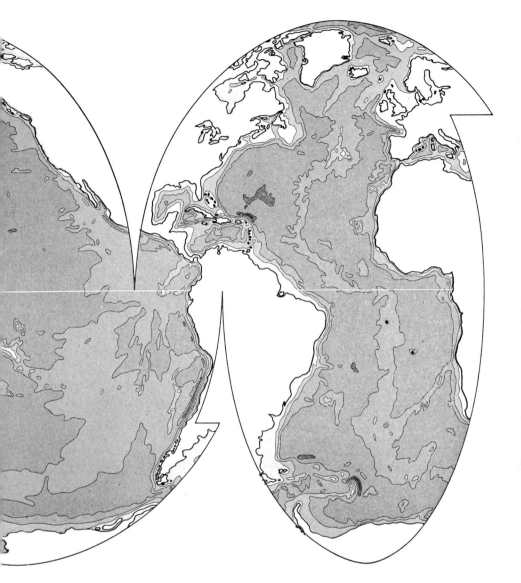

More than 70 percent of the surface of the planet Earth is covered by the sea. Its average depth is two and a half miles. To make useful charts, surveyors must make depth measurements.

and to many others on the sea bottom, Arizona's 217-mile-
long Grand Canyon is small.

The recently discovered Pacific Ocean canyon is scientifically interesting, but because of the great depth of the water
covering the canyon, it is not of practical value for navigational purposes. Although most big ships, and many small
ones, have echo sounders, their range and precision may
not be as great as that of the instruments with which oceanographic research ships are equipped. Therefore, the navigator of a commercial ship may not know when he is crossing
the canyon and cannot use it, as he does other submerged
landmarks, as a control point from which he can determine
the location of the ship.

For example, suppose a navigator approaching land after
an ocean crossing is plotting his route into port. He draws a
route line on his chart and sees that the line crosses a hilly
area on the sea bottom. The word "hills" is not printed on
the chart. They are shown by the figures on the chart telling
the depth of the water. The water is considerably shallower
over the hills than in adjacent areas, where the sea bed is
flat.

As the ship proceeds, the navigator checks the figures recorded by his echo sounder against those on his chart. He
knows that the ship is over the hills when his echo sounder
indicates a decrease in the depth of the water. He then can
measure on his route line the number of miles he must
travel to reach port. Seamen have always used visible landmarks as guides; now they can also use invisible landmarks
on the sea bottom. The development of echo sounders has
vastly increased the information charts can supply and navigators can utilize.

In spite of the many complicated instruments and techniques that today make ocean charting easier and the results more accurate, surveyors still use some rather simple

A navigator heading for San Francisco knows, by checking his chart, that he is approaching the main entrance when his echo sounder shows 20 fathoms (120 feet).

devices and procedures to obtain certain kinds of information. When a captain is selecting a spot in a harbor to anchor his boat he depends on his chart to tell him where the
harbor bottom is composed of sticky mud, in which an anchor gets a good grip, and where there are rocks over
which an anchor may skid. To provide facts about the character of a harbor bottom, surveyors must collect samples.
They do this by lowering special devices to the bottom. One
device collects a sample of the top layer of sediment; another device, called a corer, digs through a number of layers.

Surveyors "fish" for wrecks, rocks, and other isolated obstructions in coastal areas with a heavy wire cable. The
cable is dragged through the water by two boats working as
a team. This survey technique, known as a wire-drag, is
used in areas where a complete search must be made of
every foot of the sea bottom. Since a wire-drag survey takes
a long time, only a few are scheduled during a year.

No matter how carefully an area is surveyed, it can never
be checked off as finally mapped. For the shape of coasts
and the depth of the water along them are subject to change.
A storm may cut a bay in a previously straight coast or re-
shape the sea bottom so that there is shallow water where
formerly the water was deep. Today navigators are informed quickly about such changes. The first information is
frequently obtained from an aerial survey. Later, the area
may be completely rechecked by surveyors working from
boats.

The methods and equipment used for surveying the
oceans are constantly being improved, but no one has yet
devised a better design for a navigational chart than the one
developed a little more than four hundred years ago by a
Flemish map maker named Gerardus Mercator. His design
is used for most sea charts and land maps.

CHAPTER III

Portraying the Round Earth

on Flat Paper

When Gerardus Mercator tackled the problem of designing a new type of chart for navigators, he was already famous. By 1567, when Mercator began work on this project, he had been a map maker for thirty years and was recognized as the best in all Europe.

What Mercator undertook to do was to portray our spherical planet on a flat sheet of paper in such a way that a navigator could determine the direction to steer, from the place he was leaving to his destination, by drawing a straight line between them on the chart. It was impossible to find the direction of a sea route from any of the charts navigators then used.

When making a chart or a map, lines representing latitude and longitude (from the latin words meaning "width" and "length") are used as the framework. Using these lines, the map maker can place everything in its correct geographical position, which is the point at which its latitude and longitude cross.

Lines of latitude and longitude are imaginary circles used to divide the earth's surface. Since circles are measured in

Gerardus Mercator developed the framework still used for sea charts and land maps, on which a straight line drawn between two places shows the direction from one to the other.

degrees, each circle having 360 degrees, distances on lines of latitude and longitude are measured in degrees, in minutes (1/60 of a degree), and in seconds (1/60 of a minute). Thus, if we know the latitude and longitude of anything, say a lighthouse, we can accurately locate it on a map.

Lines of latitude circle the globe in an east-west direc-

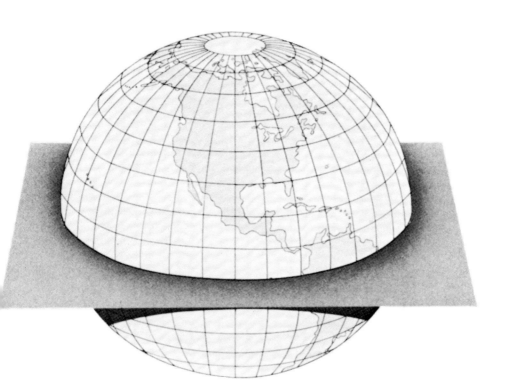

The circumference of the equator is greater than that of other circles of latitude, which become progressively smaller from the equator to the Poles.

tion. The circle of latitude midway between the North and South Poles, called the equator, divides the globe in half, or into hemispheres, one north, the other south. The circumference of the equator is greater than that of any other circle of latitude above or below it. These parallel circles become progressively smaller from the equator to the Poles.

All of the circles above the equator are called north latitude. They are numbered from the equator, which is zero degree latitude, to 90 degrees at the North Pole. (The distance from the equator to the North Pole is one fourth of a circle, or 90 degrees.) All circles of latitude below the equator are known as south latitude, and they also are numbered from the equator to 90 degrees at the South Pole.

Boston Lighthouse, equipped with one of the most pow-

erful beacons on the east coast of the United States (it is rated at 1,800,000 candle power) is located at 41 degrees, 19 minutes, and 7 seconds north latitude. During the night, ships heading for Boston Harbor after an Atlantic crossing or after making a voyage along the coast depend on Boston Lighthouse to determine their exact position.

The circles of longitude pass through the North and South Poles and are all the same length. However, as the lines curve in toward the Poles, the spaces between them become smaller. The spaces are widest at the equator and at the Poles the lines come together.

The numbering of longitude lines starts from the line that passes through Greenwich, England. Greenwich, which is on the outskirts of London, was chosen by international agreement as the place from which longitude would be reckoned because the famous Royal Observatory is located there. The numbering runs from zero, at Greenwich, to 180 degrees, halfway around the world from Greenwich. All longitude lines west of Greenwich to 180 degrees are known as west longitude. All longitude lines east of Greenwich to 180 degrees are known as east longitude. However, 180 degrees east and west longitude is the same line. It crosses the Aleutian Islands in the North Pacific and the Fiji Islands in the South Pacific.

Boston Lighthouse is located at 70 degrees, 53 minutes, and 4 seconds west longitude. Now, knowing the exact geographical address of Boston Lighthouse, we can place it in its correct position on any globe or map that is divided by latitude and longitude lines.

Latitude and longitude lines may be drawn in different ways. Both sets of lines may be curved; one set may be curved, the other slanted; and so on. The design of the framework depends on the intended use of the chart or map.

Since Mercator intended his chart to show the direction between places by a straight line, longitude and latitude had to be drawn as straight lines intersecting at right angles. But on such a framework all lines of latitude must be the same length instead of some being shorter than others, as they are on a globe, and all the spaces between the lines of longitude must be the same width.

Mercator realized that by adjusting the spaces between the lines of latitude he could create the type of framework he needed. He worked out his solution mathematically. On a Mercator chart the spaces between lines of latitude near the Poles are many times the width of those near the equator.

A map of the world drawn on Mercator's framework greatly exaggerates the size of land and ocean areas in the far north and south. For example, Greenland, which is approximately one eighth the size of South America, appears to be considerably larger than South America on a Mercator map. Every map is distorted in some way. No true representation of a sphere can be made on a flat surface. However, the distortion caused by Mercator's framework has little effect on areas in the middle latitudes, where most ships sail.

Although a Mercator chart shows a navigator the direction to steer to reach his destination, it does not show the shortest route. The shortest route on our spherical earth is, naturally, part of a circle. The length of an ocean crossing can be decreased by many miles, sometimes by hundreds of miles, by sailing what is known as a great-circle course. A good way to visualize a great circle is to cut an orange in half. The circle created on the skin by the cut is a great circle. When any sphere is cut in half through its center, the circle formed by the cut on the surface of the sphere is a great circle.

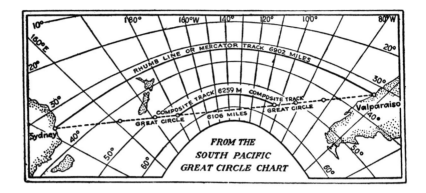

Navigators plot ocean voyages first on a great-circle chart to find the shortest route and then transfer the route to a Mercator chart to determine the direction in which to steer.

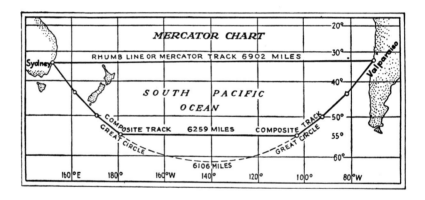

To plot a great-circle course, navigators use a special chart. Its framework is made of curved latitude lines and straight longitude lines that converge, on a chart of the Northern Hemisphere, toward the North Pole, and on a chart of the Southern Hemisphere, toward the South Pole. A straight line drawn on a great-circle chart between the ship's departure point and her destination shows the shortest route, but not the direction to steer it.

Thus, for ocean crossings navigators need two charts of

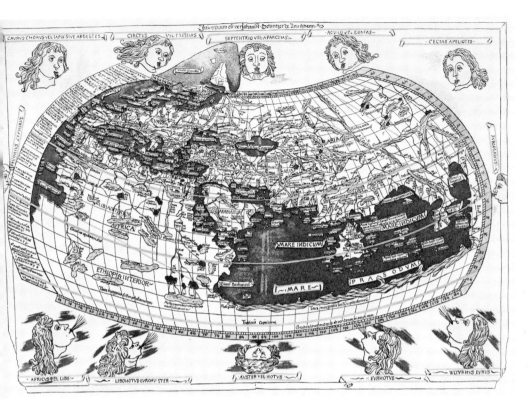

Ptolemy's map does not show the vastness of the world's oceans and misled Columbus as to the distance he would have to sail to reach India.

the same area: a great-circle chart to determine the shortest route and a Mercator chart to find its direction. First, the navigator draws the route he has plotted on the great-circle chart and then he divides the route into sections. Next, using the longitude and latitude lines as guides, he transfers each section to the Mercator chart. The navigator can then determine the direction to steer on each section of his route.

The top of a Mercator chart is north, the bottom south; to the right is east and to the left, west. The custom of orienting maps in this way was established about eighteen hundred years ago by the Egyptian geographer, Claudius Ptolemy, on whose calculations Columbus relied. But merely knowing the direction of the four cardinal points is

not enough for plotting a course. It may be part way between north and east, or part way between any other two
cardinal points. To enable navigators to determine the exact
direction to steer, one or more compass roses are printed on
each Mercator chart.

A compass rose is a circle divided, like the card in a compass, by short lines, each indicating a specific direction. In
former days the roses on charts were elaborately designed
and beautifully colored. Gold and silver, in addition to vivid
colored inks, were used. Portolan charts (from *porto*, the
Italian word for port) were crisscrossed by lines colored to
match the points of the rose through which they passed.
The lines showed the direction to ports.

On modern American charts of coastal waters compass
roses are printed in purplish red. The rose consists of an
inner and an outer circle; each has its own zero, or north,
line. The zero line on the outer circle, topped by a star,
shows the direction of true north. The zero line on the inner
circle, topped by an arrow, indicates north as a magnetic
compass will show it in the area covered by the chart. In
some places the earth's magnetic force causes the needle of
a magnetic compass to point east (to the right) of true
north, in other places, west (to the left) of true north.

The result is similar to a clock that is five minutes fast or

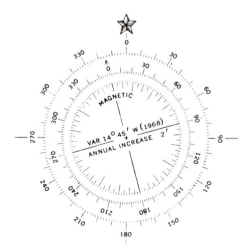

*The star on the outer circle of a compass rose shows the direction
of true north; the arrow on the inner circle shows magnetic north.*

This portolan chart of the Mediterranean Sea, engraved in 1597, is a copy of one made about two hundred years earlier.

five minutes slow. The error does not affect a single hour but all hours. The way a magnetic compass shows north affects the way it shows all directions.

Before Columbus made his first voyage to America, navigators knew only that a magnetic compass might point to the right of north, and some compasses were adjusted to eliminate this error. Columbus discovered that a compass may also err to the left of north. Five days after leaving the Azores, a group of islands located about 800 miles from Portugal, the needle of his compass began to point to the left of north.

Other explorers had similar compass trouble while crossing the Atlantic. When they could see the North Star (which is almost directly above the North Pole), they could calculate the allowance to make for the difference between true north as shown by the star and north according to their magnetic compass. But there was no way of checking during stormy periods when the star was hidden by clouds.

Seafarers learned that the extent to which their magnetic compasses varied from true north was not the same in all parts of the Atlantic. As ships sailed back and forth between Europe and America, captains noted the extent of

the variation along their routes. As early as 1530 these records were used to make a chart showing how a compass
could be expected to act in various parts of the Atlantic.

Now the U. S. Naval Oceanographic Office uses planes as
well as ships to collect data about magnetic variation. In addition to the information for specific areas printed on Mercator charts, the United States publishes special charts
showing world-wide magnetic conditions. Because the
earth's magnetic force changes, new editions of these charts
are published every five years.

Many ships are now equipped with the kind of compass
called a "gyro" compass. Such a compass points to true
north. When a navigator uses a gyro to steer by, he gets the
direction of his course in coastal waters by lining it up with
the outer circle of a compass rose on his Mercator chart of
the area. When steering by a magnetic compass, the course
to sail is lined up with the inner circle of the compass rose.
During ocean voyages, a navigator steering by a magnetic
compass must figure the correction to make for its variation
from true north. Lines printed on ocean charts show the extent of the variation in different areas.

A navigational chart contains a tremendous amount of
information, but, unlike an automobile road map (which is
also made on Mercator's design), it is not labeled with the
number of miles between places. Seafarers must figure mile-
age for themselves.

The unit for measuring distance is one minute of latitude,
as shown on the side borders of a Mercator chart. One minute of latitude equals one sea mile. In olden times seamen
used a league as the measure of distance, but a league was
not standardized and might mean two miles or four. Now,
by international agreement, the length of a sea (nautical)
mile has been established at 6076.10 feet. It is about one-
seventh longer than a land mile.

On some charts a sea mile looks very small. When a chart

covers a large area everything is shown on a small scale. One inch on such a chart may represent 50 or more sea miles. A navigator uses a small-scale chart to get a general picture of a coast. But when preparing to enter a harbor, he uses a chart on which an inch may represent less than half a mile. Such a large-scale chart gives detailed information about the varying depths of the water in the harbor, the kind of sediment on the harbor bottom (pebbles, sand, rocks, coral, and so on), and indicates positions of anchored markers (called buoys) at channels and danger spots, lighthouses, and prominent buildings and piers on shore.

Charts are designed to make the information printed on them stand out clearly. However, the only way that all the facts can be shown is by using abbreviations and code symbols. To read a navigational chart one must understand the abbreviations and be able to decipher the code symbols. The key to abbreviations and symbols is printed in a booklet entitled Chart No. 1. A copy can be ordered from the National Ocean Survey's office in Washington, D. C. Experienced navigators keep Chart No. 1 handy and refer to it whenever in doubt about the meaning of an abbreviation or a symbol. It is their dictionary of terms.

On an automobile map, a town, mountain, or lake may be shown a little to one side or another of its exact geographical position; this does not matter to most motorists. But a navigator must know positions exactly. If a chart shows a submerged rock fifty feet from its actual position, a navigator may run his ship onto the rock. Such groundings have occurred.

How do surveyors gathering the facts for a chart determine exact locations? The answer is that they use land positions as the base for their measurements. When charting the sea, everything is pinpointed in relationship to some feature on land. Therefore, before an accurate sea chart can be made, the land must be accurately mapped.

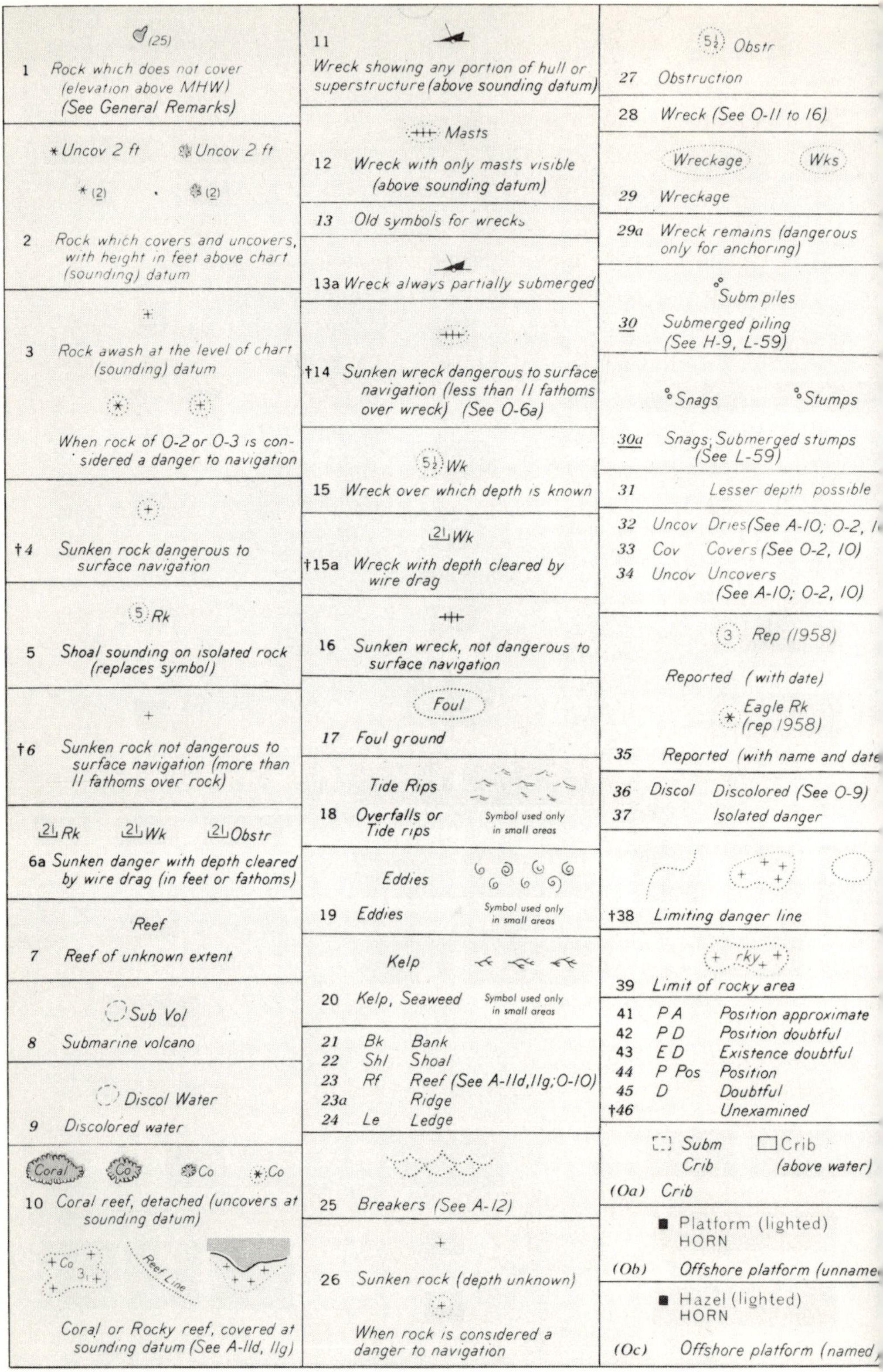
(25)
1 Rock which does not cover (elevation above MHW) (See General Remarks)
Uncov 2 ft
Uncov 2 ft
(2)
(2)
2 Rock which covers and uncovers, with height in feet above chart (sounding) datum
3 Rock awash at the level of chart (sounding) datum
When rock of O-2 or O-3 is considered a danger to navigation
†4 Sunken rock dangerous to surface navigation
5 Rk
5 Shoal sounding on isolated rock (replaces symbol)
†6 Sunken rock not dangerous to surface navigation (more than 11 fathoms over rock)
21 Rk
21 Wk
21 Obstr
6a Sunken danger with depth cleared by wire drag (in feet or fathoms)
Reef
7 Reef of unknown extent
Sub Vol
8 Submarine volcano
Discol Water
9 Discolored water
Coral
Co
Co
Co
10 Coral reef, detached (uncovers at sounding datum)
Co
3
Reef Line
Coral or Rocky reef, covered at sounding datum (See A-11d, 11g)
11
Wreck showing any portion of hull or superstructure (above sounding datum)
Masts
12 Wreck with only masts visible (above sounding datum)
13 Old symbols for wrecks
13a Wreck always partially submerged
†14 Sunken wreck dangerous to surface navigation (less than 11 fathoms over wreck) (See O-6a)
5½ Wk
15 Wreck over which depth is known
21 Wk
†15a Wreck with depth cleared by wire drag
16 Sunken wreck, not dangerous to surface navigation
Foul
17 Foul ground
Tide Rips
18 Overfalls or Tide rips
Symbol used only in small areas
Eddies
19 Eddies
Symbol used only in small areas
Kelp
20 Kelp, Seaweed
Symbol used only in small areas
21 Bk Bank
22 Shl Shoal
23 Rf Reef (See A-11d, 11g; O-10)
23a Ridge
24 Le Ledge
25 Breakers (See A-12)
26 Sunken rock (depth unknown)
When rock is considered a danger to navigation
5½ Obstr
27 Obstruction
28 Wreck (See O-11 to 16)
Wreckage
Wks
29 Wreckage
29a Wreck remains (dangerous only for anchoring)
Subm piles
30 Submerged piling (See H-9, L-59)
Snags
Stumps
30a Snags; Submerged stumps (See L-59)
31 Lesser depth possible
32 Uncov Dries (See A-10; O-2,
33 Cov Covers (See O-2, 10)
34 Uncov Uncovers (See A-10; O-2, 10)
3 Rep (1958)
Reported (with date)
Eagle Rk (rep 1958)
35 Reported (with name and date
36 Discol Discolored (See O-9)
37 Isolated danger
†38 Limiting danger line
rky
39 Limit of rocky area
41 PA Position approximate
42 PD Position doubtful
43 ED Existence doubtful
44 P Pos Position
45 D Doubtful
†46 Unexamined
Subm Crib
Crib (above water)
(Oa) Crib
Platform (lighted) HORN
(Ob) Offshore platform (unname
Hazel (lighted) HORN
(Oc) Offshore platform (named

To understand the meaning of the abbreviations and symbols used on charts, navigators refer to a booklet entitled Chart No. 1.

CHAPTER IV

The Importance of

Triangles

When Congress authorized the charting of the coastal waters of the United States in 1807, captains and ship owners expected that they would soon have the charts they had been asking for. But nearly ten years elapsed before the work was started. Lack of funds was one reason for the delay. Then, after money was appropriated, plans for the survey were disrupted by the War of 1812.

When the work finally was begun, there were complaints about the way it was being handled. Ferdinand R. Hassler, the surveyor appointed by President Jefferson, seemed to mariners to be neglecting his job. He was concentrating on land surveys and was paying no attention to water areas.

But Hassler had been chosen to take charge of the bureau, named the Survey of the Coast (now the National Ocean Survey), just because his plan provided for starting on land. There had been many well-qualified applicants for the post of superintendent of the survey (James Madison was one of them), and each had submitted his proposed method of operation. When the proposals were considered, President Jefferson was most favorably impressed by

From Life on Stone

A. Gerdevich
1842

F. R. Haßler

F.R. HASSLER.

Superintendent of the U.S. Coast Survey
1807–1843

Ferdinand R. Hassler, appointed by President Thomas Jefferson
to survey the east coast of the United States, had a stormy career
but lived to see the value of his work recognized.

Hassler's. The President understood that to chart the sea it was necessary first to map the coast.

Hassler started in the vicinity of New York Harbor, where he established a base line. The first step when mapping land that has not previously been accurately surveyed is to measure, precisely, a base line. It serves as a primary reference for subsequent mapping. Such a base line may be many miles long. Whenever possible, a level stretch of land is chosen for a base line and the points where it is to start and end are marked. Then the surveyors determine the geographic location of the beginning of the line. Hassler did this by measuring the height of a number of bright stars above the horizon and their compass direction. Navigators use the same method during an ocean crossing to find the exact location of their ship. To achieve an exact result, Hassler took many more star sights than navigators ordinarily do. Modern surveyors may compute sights on as many as a hundred stars to locate the origin point of a base line.

After Hassler had calculated the latitude and longitude of the point where his base line was to begin, he determined the location of the point where it was to end by measuring the distance between the two points and by noting the compass direction between them.

In Hassler's time surveyors used chains for measuring. The chains were made up of a hundred bars, each 7.92 inches long, making a chain of exactly 66 feet. Surveyors stretched their chain over a base line many times to make sure their measurements were accurate.

Today, instead of measuring with a chain, an electronic instrument is often used to determine the length of a base line. One device projects a beam of light from one end of a base line to a reflector at the other end and calculates the length of the line from the time required for the light to

be reflected back. Another type of device calculates distance by transmitting a radio signal and timing the return of its echo. The government now specifies that no error greater than half an inch in the measurement of each mile of base line is acceptable.

From one measured base line many points can be accurately mapped by using a method called triangulation. This is a practical application of a mathematical principle discovered long ago: if you know the length of one side of a triangle and the size of two of its angles, the lengths of the

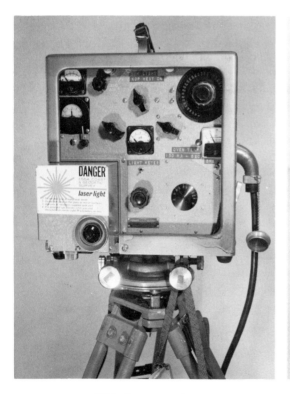 

This laser geodimeter measures base lines precisely by projecting a light ray from one end of the line to the 14-prism reflector at the other end of the line.

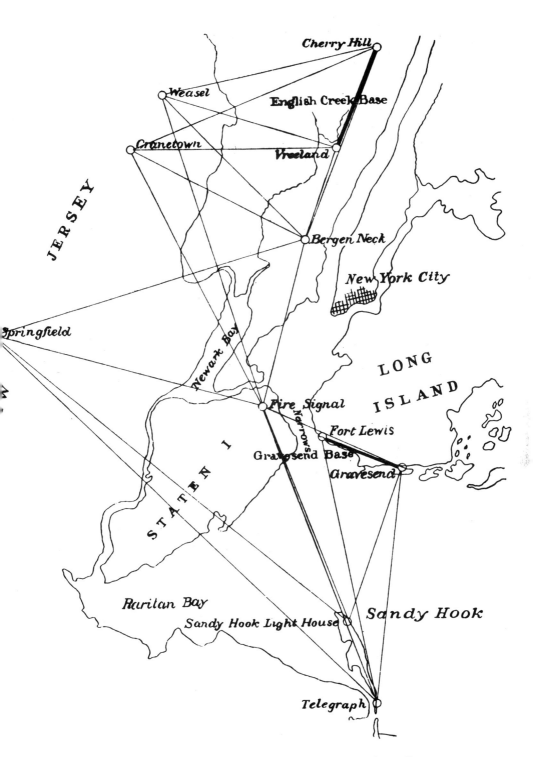

Hassler spent two years (1816–1817) measuring two base lines and completing a network of triangulations. The United States Congress wanted the surveying done more rapidly.

second and third sides of the triangle can be calculated
without measuring them. Most mapping is done by triangulation.

As an example, assume that after establishing a base line,
the surveyors wish to determine the location of a radio
tower some miles away. The surveyors carefully place their
angle-measuring instrument (called a theodolite) at point A,
the beginning of the base line. Then a surveyor focuses the
instrument's telescope and sights the radio tower through it.
The angle formed by the sight line to the tower and the base
line is read from the scale on the instrument. After the instrument has been moved to the other end of the base line,
point B, the surveyor again takes a sight on the radio tower
and notes the angle between this second sight line and the
base line.

Now, knowing the size of the two angles and the exact
length of the base line, a surveyor can calculate the length
of the two sight lines that form the sides of the triangle.
From a series of calculations the location of the radio tower
is determined. Also, the calculations provide the surveyors
with two additional lines of known length, which can be
used as base lines for determining the location of other
structures or points. Similarly, the sides of the second and
third triangles provide bases for more triangles. There is no
limit to the number of triangles that surveyors can develop
from one measured base line.

As a check on the accuracy of the mapping, usually more
than one measured base line is used. Points located by triangulation from one measured base line are located from another measured base line. Hassler measured two base lines
and completed a small net of triangles. He spent two years
on this work. Because legislators of that day were relatively
uninformed on the need for such precision in geodetic surveying, Congress decided that the authorized survey of the

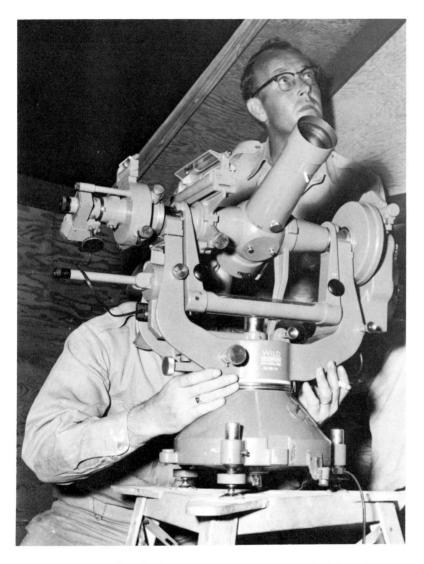

An astronomic theodolite used to measure the height of stars. Sights on as many as a hundred stars may be computed to locate the origin point of a base line.

A tall pole erected at the end of a base line is draped with cloth to make the marker easier to see. The effect is a tentlike appearance.

coast was taking far too much time to complete. Therefore, Hassler was dismissed.

Little progress was made in mapping the land or in charting the sea until 1832, when Hassler was reappointed chief of the coast survey. In the next eleven years he and his staff extended the triangulation net eastward from New York to Rhode Island and southward to Maryland. Sixteen hundred miles of the coast were mapped in detail. Surveying of water areas finally began in 1834. In addition to discovering many dangerous underwater hazards, the surveyors found a previously unknown deepwater channel that is still used by ships heading for New York or departing from it. The channel was named Gedney, in honor of Lt. T. R. Gedney, commander of the survey schooner from which the waterway was discovered.

Today it is not necessary to measure base lines prior to resurveying the coastal waters of the United States. The National Ocean Survey has a record of the precise geographic location of thousands of points, and any two, convenient for the surveyors' purpose, can be used as the beginning and end of a base line. The length of the line can be computed because the latitude and longitude of the points are known. Tall poles, 20 to 30 feet high, or portable towers are often erected at the two ends of a base line. Sometimes cloth is draped over the poles to make them easier to see from the surveyors' boat. If you spend a vacation at the shore and see something that looks like a high tent, it is probably a marker erected by surveyors working in the area.

Suppose that, while probing the sea bottom, surveyors discover a rock covered by comparatively shallow water. The simplest method for determining the location of the rock so that it can be correctly shown on charts is for the surveyors to anchor their boat over the rock. The surveyors determine the position of their boat (and of the rock) by a procedure

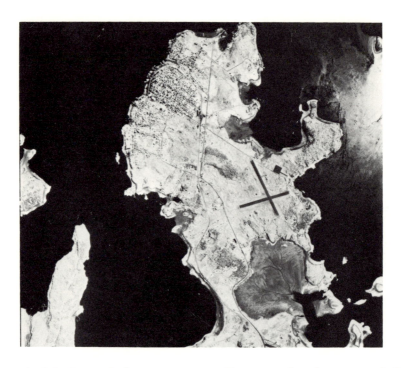

Aerial views of the same areas. Compare the sharpness of the

that is the reverse of the one used to locate an object from a base line. The surveyors focus their sighting instrument first on the pole marking one end of their base line on shore and then on the pole marking the other end of the line. The instrument shows the compass direction from the boat to the two ends of the base line. When the sight lines are drawn on plotting paper, the point at which they cross is the location of the surveyors' boat and also, of course, of the rock.

Surveyors working beyond sight of land pinpoint the position of their finds by tuning in radio signals from special transmitters erected at the two ends of a base line. The radio signals enable surveyors to plot lines to the transmitters. It does not matter how many hundreds of miles the

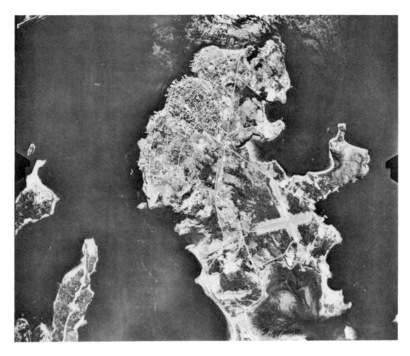

infrared film with the picture to the right made on ordinary black-and-white film.

lines represent; the surveyors' ship is at the spot where the two lines cross.

Coastal charts include a map of the shore and mapping it used to be difficult. Surveyors were obliged to scramble over rocks and plod through mud and sand, measuring and sketching the curves and varying heights of the land. Now much of this information is obtained from analysis of aerial photographs.

Preliminary measurements of the depth of water are also being made from aerial photographs. Pictures made on color film indicate depth by variations in the shade of the water. The deepest water photographs as blue-violet. Color film can "see through" water to the sea floor and show its

contours and formations. The depth to which the film can penetrate depends on how clear the water is.

Tremendous advances in photographic surveying have been made in recent years. The cameras used for this type of surveying fit into openings in the plane's fuselage and face straight down to the land or sea below. They are operated by an automatic timing device, which may be set to take as many as 15 photographs a minute.

Each film, after the first, shows part of the area on the preceding film. The overlapping may amount to as much as 60 percent. When the first two films, or the second and third films, or any succeeding pair are examined in a stereoscopic viewer, they give a three-dimensional perspective. The chart maker can then measure how high objects are in addition to determining their exact locations.

In order to do this, each pair of films must contain control stations, things whose latitude, longitude, and height are known. These stations provide the chart maker with a reference and a basis for his measurements. If it were necessary to send out a surveying party to establish the location of only one control station for each pair of pictures, photographic mapping would be impractical.

The problem is solved by the overlapping of the pictures. To understand the technique, assume that only one control station is needed for each pair of pictures. (Actually, six are considered necessary.) The first pair of pictures that the chart maker examines in his viewer contains a lighthouse. It stands out clearly. The location and height of the lighthouse, like that of all others, is listed in official records. Therefore the lighthouse can be used as a control station from which the positions of other prominent structures in the pictures can be calculated. Suppose that another structure shown is a church.

After completing work on pictures one and two, the chart maker examines pictures two and three. This pair does not include the lighthouse but shows the church. Because its position and height have been determined from the position and measurement of the lighthouse, the chart maker can now use the church as a control station from which other prominent landmarks can be located. Pictures three and four do not show the church but include objects that the chart maker has previously located from the church. Thus, by overlapping the photographs, there are control stations in each pair on which measurements can be based.

Mapping from aerial photographs is a good deal more difficult than this simplified explanation makes it seem. As a matter of fact, the mathematics involved in the procedure are so complicated that computers are now used to obtain the answers required to plot positions correctly.

Ordinarily, it is not necessary, prior to photographing the coasts of the United States, for the surveyors to determine the latitude, longitude, or height of the control stations because these facts are known from previous surveys.

However, there are many parts of the world that have never been accurately surveyed. In these areas charting coastal waters is a pioneer project. The surveyors must start, just as Hassler did, by measuring a base line. Surveyors of the Naval Oceanographic Office often undertake such projects. The United States has co-operated with many nations that have requested assistance in charting the water bordering their shores. Sometimes the men who do the preliminary land surveying work on rocky, uninhabited coasts and sometimes in jungles. When an agreement was made with the Philippine government to chart its coastal waters, much of the groundwork was done in thick jungles.

U. S. Navy surveyors worked in the dense jungles of Luzon, the largest of the Philippine Islands, before beginning the charting of the Philippine coastal waters.

CHAPTER V

A Survey

Expedition

Until the surveyors went into the jungles of Luzon, the largest of the Philippine Islands, they did not know how difficult carrying out their assignment was going to be. When it was being discussed, representatives of the Philippine government said that some of the land had previously been surveyed and that there were many marked points whose longitude and latitude had been determined. But the American surveyors found few markers; most had disappeared under the thickly intertwined plants, bushes, vines, and trees of the jungle. In addition, markers that still were visible appeared to have shifted. The surveyors had no choice: they had to start anew. They began by establishing base lines and then, by triangulation, mapped the land.

Among the points whose precise position was calculated were three on islands where radio transmitters were to be erected. During the charting of Luzon's offshore waters the survey ship would depend on directional signals, broadcast from the islands, to keep on course and to determine the location of everything that the probing of the water disclosed. Just as surveyors working near shore use visible markers for

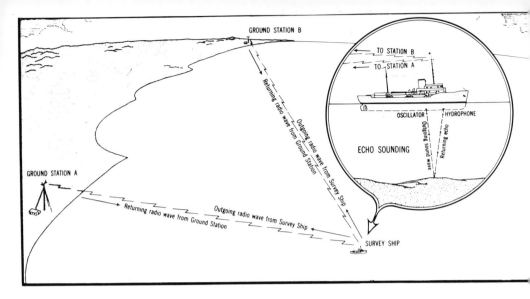

Within the image: GROUND STATION B, TO STATION B, TO STATION A, OSCILLATOR, HYDROPHONE, ECHO SOUNDING, Outgoing sound wave, Returning echo, Returning radio wave from Ground Station, Outgoing radio wave from Survey Ship, GROUND STATION A, Returning radio wave from Ground Station, Outgoing radio wave from Survey Ship, SURVEY SHIP

When working beyond sight of land, survey ships depend on signals from radio stations whose exact location is known. The ship's position is determined from the signals.

the exact navigation required during a charting operation, so surveyors working offshore base their measurements on radioed signals. Such measurements can be accurate only if the location of the transmitting station is known.

The sites selected for the stations were on the tops of steep islands with rocky shores. Height is advantageous for the transmission of radio signals because it extends the signal's range. However, during the surveying operation, the height of the islands and their rocky shores created practical difficulties when supplies had to be delivered by boat. Ordinarily supplies were transported by helicopter. It took only one hour for the copter to bring in a fifteen-day supply of everything needed by the men operating the radio station. Full supplies included eight barrels of drinking water, fifteen cases of food, and five drums of diesel oil for the electric generators that produced the power for broadcasting. Once, while the helicopter was being repaired, supplies had to be sent to one of the islands and a small shipment was transported by boat. Carrying the containers ashore

was difficult and it took the radiomen five hours to lug the supplies up the steep trail to their camp.

The Navy designated its veteran survey ship *Maury* to collect data for charts of the Philippines' offshore waters. The ship was named for Matthew Fontaine Maury, a pioneer in charting the seas. The survey ship started her expedition from the naval base at Pearl Harbor, Honolulu.

The *Maury* is a large ship; her length is 426 feet and her width, 58 feet. Near the stern, on the top deck, there is a landing pad for a helicopter. The *Maury*'s copter landed shortly before the time set for the ship's departure and was securely lashed in place so that it would not shift and be damaged during the ocean voyage.

The helicopter was vital for the success of the survey operation. In addition to airlifting thousands of tons of equipment and supplies from the ship to bases ashore, it was also used for aerial mapping.

Among the boats on the *Maury*'s top deck were two "soundboats," each about 50 feet long. From the outside, a soundboat looks much the same as a motorboat that sportsmen use, but inside it is very different. Instead of being comfortably furnished with chairs and berths, the cabin of a soundboat is filled with electronic equipment. Soundboats survey the water near shore while the mother ship works miles offshore.

If you were to go aboard the *Maury,* or any other survey ship, you would think you were visiting a laboratory. The most desirable cabin space in survey ships is not used for living accommodations, as it is on passenger liners, but for workrooms. One of the largest rooms in the *Maury* is its electronic headquarters. Instruments are fastened to the floor, to the walls—even to the ceiling. (The nautical terms for these locations are deck, bulkheads, and overhead.)

Of all the instruments, the most prominent are the echo

The Maury *departs for a survey expedition carrying soundboats for surveying near shore and a helicopter for aerial mapping and airlifting equipment.*

sounders. The *Maury*'s precision sounders show their measurements on dials and, in addition, automatically draw a profile picture of the sea bottom. The depth of the water can be read from the drawing.

Scientists who staff a survey ship are busy from the beginning of a voyage to the end. While en route to the area that is to be charted, the scientists test samples of the water through which the ship travels. Detailed records are kept of the variations in the temperature, salinity, and chemical composition of the water, and of weather conditions. Information about the upper air is obtained at regular intervals (usually every 12 hours) by sending aloft radiosonde balloons. The balloons carry instruments that measure temperature, humidity, and air pressure and automatically transmit these measurements to the ship. At all times during an ocean crossing the depth of the water on the ship's route is recorded.

Soon after the *Maury* arrived in Manila Bay, the sound-boats were launched and the men assigned to operate them went aboard. They headed for the pier where the boats were to be based. Preparing the soundboats for surveying did not take long.

The situation was different on the *Maury*. There were many preliminary jobs before the ship could begin charting. The radio transmitters had to be unloaded and erected on the three islands. Then, after the transmitters were operative, the *Maury* had to make test runs to check the reception of the directional signals. As on all seagoing ships, the men of the *Maury* worked in shifts, or watches, as sailors say. At quitting time for one shift, another started work. Thus the operation of the ship continued 24 hours a day.

One of the first charts for which the *Maury* collected information was to be drawn on a small scale. Each 0.15 of an inch on the chart would represent one sea mile. On such a small-scale chart comparatively few details are shown.

While collecting data for this chart, the depth of the water and the location of the ship were recorded in a book at fifteen-minute intervals. When the man watching the clock called "mark," two instruments were checked simultaneously. The depth of the water was read from the echo sounder and the location of the ship from the receiver tuned in on the radio transmitters on the islands. In the future, fully automatic instruments will eliminate the need for men to stand watch and keep records. Locations and depths will be recorded in computer language.

During one part of the survey, when the *Maury* was probing an area over a dangerous coral reef about which detailed information was required, the ship's location and the depth of the water were noted at five-minute intervals. From these data it was found that the reef extended two miles farther north than was indicated on the old chart. Perhaps this

error explains a shipwreck that occurred shortly before the *Maury* began its survey. A large freighter grounded on the reef and could not be budged.

The most dangerous hours for the *Maury* were when she was caught in a typhoon. "Phyllis," the name given the typhoon by weathermen, hit in December. The storm was detected by the *Maury*'s radar (*ra*dio *d*etection *a*nd *r*anging). From the picture on the radar screen it was estimated that the ship was about 20 miles from the center of the storm. One side of a typhoon is more dangerous than the other; the *Maury* was on the more dangerous side. Soon the ship was battling 35-foot waves. The *Maury*'s captain decided that his best chance to escape was by executing the tricky maneuver of passing through the center of the typhoon to its less dangerous side. While approaching the center, or eye, of the storm, mountainous waves struck from all directions and at times the ship made no headway. But finally she fought her way out of the storm.

Immediately after discovering the typhoon, the *Maury* radioed the Navy's nearest weather station, which broadcast warnings to ships and coastal communities in the path of the storm. Because of these warnings Phyllis caused fewer casualties and less damage than it otherwise might have. People evacuated coastal areas and ships scurried away from the storm.

Bad weather hampered the *Maury*'s surveying operations at other times, but the choppy waves in Manila Bay were a daily problem for the soundboats charting the water near shore. The surveyors realized, shortly after beginning their assignment, that they would have to start work soon after sunrise and stop early in the afternoon. In the morning Manila Bay is smooth, but in the afternoon the wind blows hard and the water becomes so rough that the helmsmen of the soundboats could not maintain a true course.

Samples of the sea bottom are obtained by lowering a spring-triggered device that takes a bite from the bottom and then snaps shut.

When making a survey, boats follow a specified plan. For a chart of offshore waters the plan may provide that probing be done on courses spaced one mile apart. But for a harbor chart, on which many details are given, the specified distance between courses may be only 50 yards. The first course is usually run close to shore. The boat starts at one side of the harbor and, paralleling the shore, travels to the other side. It then goes out the specified distance for the next course and proceeds to cross the harbor again. The boat continues to travel back and forth across the harbor in a series of equally spaced parallel lines until it has covered the area to be surveyed. Then the surveyors start another series of courses at right angles to the first. While charting Manila Bay, the men on the soundboats kept a minute-by-minute record of the depth of the water and the location of the boat.

Maintaining such a schedule is a strain, and the interruption was welcomed when the boat stopped to secure bottom samples of the harbor. A device known as a snapper was used. It has two spring-triggered, clamshell-shaped jaws that bite into the bottom and then snap shut, locking in the sample. If a snapper lands on rock it is empty when pulled up.

After the soundboats completed each day's survey, there still remained a considerable amount of work that had to be done. All the notations had to be plotted in their proper locations on a large sheet of mapping paper, called a "boat sheet." But before doing this, every one of the depth figures had to be corrected for the stage of the tide at the time the depth measurement was taken. This information is obtained from tide gauges, which record the changing depth of the sea as the tide rises and falls. If there is no tide gauge in a harbor that is to be surveyed, the surveyors install one and calibrate it.

A recording tide gauge draws a graph of the changing depth of the sea as the tide rises and falls. All depths measured near shore are adjusted for tidal changes.

Most harbor charts are based on the depth of the water at average low tide. Therefore, if a soundboat's measurement was made when the water was five feet above the low-tide level, five feet must be subtracted from the figure given by the boat's depth sounder. Precise calculations are required for each depth figure. Formerly, all the figuring was done by surveyors making the correction computations with pencil and paper; now this job is done largely by computers.

The *Maury* spent about six months on the Philippine survey and then completed other assignments in the Pacific. After twenty-three years of service as a survey ship, the *Maury* was retired in 1969. The Navy sometimes gives the same name to a new ship that an old one carried, and at some future date a new oceanographic research ship may be named *Maury* and sail forth to continue the exploration of the sea.

Ships heading for Boston harbor use this lighthouse as a guide. Boston Light, as it is named, has a powerful beacon that is visible for miles.

CHAPTER VI

Wreck Hunting

Thousands of wrecked ships—passenger steamers, cargo carriers, and warships—dot the sea bottom near the coasts of the United States. Some of the ships went down hundreds of years ago. Two that tantalize underwater treasure hunters are British warships that sank during the Revolutionary War. One of the ships went to the bottom near the Delaware coast, the other in the part of New York Harbor called Hell Gate, where there are swirling currents and many rocks. Both warships are believed to have been carrying large quantities of gold for paying the British army. A number of schemes have been developed for recovering the gold, but none has been successful.

Undersea treasure hunts, even when unsuccessful, are usually reported in detail. But so little news is given about the wreck-hunting expeditions of the National Ocean Survey that few people know anything whatever about these operations. Yet they are of greater importance than diving for treasure, and, in many respects, equally intriguing.

Most of the government's wreck hunting is done to make sea travel safe. Some wrecks project so close to the surface that if a ship tried to pass over them it might collide with the wreck and sink.

The government experts who search for sunken ships often are referred to as "wrecking crews." Actually, they hunt for all types of obstructions. The method used was originally developed to locate rocks that during some up-heaval in bygone times had been strewn here and there on the sea floor. During a regular survey, the bottom is searched only along the path that the surveyors' boat travels, but wrecking crews comb every foot of the whole area in which they are working. They do this by dragging a heavy wire over the sea bottom. Two boats work together in wire-dragging. One end of the wire is fastened to each boat. The boats are then steered on parallel courses, towing the wire behind them.

The wire may be very long. For instance, during a recent wire-drag survey in the Gulf of Mexico the wire used was about two miles long. The area searched extended for 150 miles along the shore and 60 miles out from it. There were at least 50 wrecks known to be in the area. The wire-dragging boats worked more than a year in the Gulf. Wire-

Two boats are needed for a wire-drag survey. Weights are fastened to the wire, making it sink to the depth to be explored for wrecks and other obstructions on the bottom.

dragging is slow work; the average speed of a wire-dragging boat is less than two miles an hour.

Weights are attached to the wire to make it sink to the depth specified for the survey. The wire may be weighted to sink 350 feet or 35 feet, depending on the depth of the water in the area and the purpose for which the wire-drag survey is being made. In one area that was to be used for submarine trials, the wire was dragged 350 feet below the surface to make certain that the water was free of obstructions to the depth at which the dives and speed tests were to be conducted.

A number of floats are fastened to the wire with cords long enough to allow the floats to rise to the surface, no matter how far below it the wire may be. The floats serve as telltales; they show when the wire has made a "catch."

Until it does, the wire forms an arc behind the two boats towing it. The curve of the wire is mirrored by the floats. When the wire snags on an obstruction, it is pulled into a V. The obstruction is at the point of the V. Lookouts on each of the wire-dragging boats watch the floats and, as soon as they begin to move into a V, signal for a reduction in speed. The boats maintain just enough forward movement to hold the wire taut so that it cannot slip off from whatever it has caught.

Meanwhile, a boat called a "tender," which accompanies the wire-draggers, heads for the point of the V. After anchoring a marker at the point, the wire is freed, and while the wire-draggers proceed with their search, the men on the tender measure the depth of the water over the obstruction and also determine its location.

Ordinarily, when working beyond sight of land, locations are determined from radioed navigational signals. However, during the Gulf of Mexico survey visible markers were used. In the Gulf there are many undersea oil wells, each topped by a high skeleton tower in which the pumping equipment is housed. Oil companies are licensed to pump

A "wrecking crew" reeling out a wire during a survey operation. The weighted part of the wire is underwater, astern of the boat.

oil from a specified area and must file with the government the exact location of their pumping structures. The towers therefore made perfect bases from which the surveyors could determine the position of obstructions on which their wire snagged.

For charting purposes, the most important thing to determine about an obstruction is the depth of the water covering it. If a wire is being dragged 50 feet below the surface when it catches, the surveyors know only that there is something 50 feet down. How much higher does the obstruction project? A diver is often sent to find out. After scouting around the obstruction, he holds the bottom end of a measuring line at what appears to him to be the obstruction's highest point. A surveyor on the boat holds the other end of the measuring line and reads from it the distance between the top of the obstruction and the surface.

Wire-draggers have another technique for finding the highest point of an obstruction. They remove some of the weights from the wire, which then, being lighter, rises a certain number of feet. The wire is again dragged over the obstruction, and, if it does not catch, the surveyors know that the top of the obstruction is below the new level of the wire. Adjusting the weights on a wire is not an easy job and sometimes it must be done more than once to find the highest point of an obstruction.

A wire-dragging expedition is responsible only for locating obstructions, not for removing them. However, after the wreck of an old ship with high masts was found in New York harbor, divers were sent down to remove the masts. The ship, like many other wrecks, had settled on the bottom in an upright position, and the projecting masts were close enough to the surface to be a navigational danger. The wreck was found during a search for five barges loaded with railroad cars that had gone to the bottom after a collision

with a steamer. The approximate location of the collision was known, but, although wire-draggers searched every foot of the area, only four of the barges were found. The disappearance of the fifth is an unsolved mystery.

Wrecks are sometimes hunted with electronic devices. One called sonar (from *so*und *na*vigation *a*nd *r*anging) is giving good results. Like echo sounders that measure the depth of the water under a boat, sonar equipment consists of a transmitter that sends a sound signal and a receiver that picks up the echo. Transmissions from echo sounders travel vertically, whereas sonar signals can be directed ahead of the boat, in back of it, or to either side. Sonar is used in much the same way as you use a flashlight when walking along a dark road to illuminate surrounding areas.

An experienced operator can tell from the echo, or "ping," of a sonar signal the type of obstruction it has hit. The echo from a rock is different from that of a steel ship. A few years ago a lightship that sank near the Massachusetts coast during a hurricane was located by sonar. (Lightships serve the same purpose as lighthouses and are anchored in places where, because of the depth of the water or for other reasons, a permanent structure cannot be erected.) After the sonar operator reported an obstruction that he believed was the lightship, divers verified the find. Wire-draggers then went to work and found that the highest point of the wreck was 50 feet below the surface.

The lightship, like most sunken ships, will not be raised. Its grave will be shown on charts. The divers, members of a diving club, salvaged some of the lightship's equipment, including a bell weighing nearly a ton. The bell was used while the lightship was on station to sound warnings to passing ships during foggy weather. The bell is now on display at the Cape Cod National Seashore Maritime Museum at Eastham, Massachusetts.

This bell, which weighs nearly a ton, was salvaged by divers from a sunken lightship and is now on display at the Cape Cod National Seashore Museum.

CHAPTER VII

Tracking

Ocean Currents

More than 16,000 tightly corked bottles containing
stamped, self-addressed postcards have been found, in recent years, on Atlantic Ocean beaches in America and Europe. A brief printed message on the cards requested that a
person who picked up a bottle state where and when he
found it and return the card. The bottles, of the kind ordinarily used for soft drinks, had been thrown into the Atlantic between Florida and the Gulf of St. Lawrence from ships
and aircraft. Seafarers and flyers had performed this service
at the request of scientists who were studying currents.

When you watch the sea it seems as though waves push
the water forward, but this is an illusion. Except when
waves roll up on shore, they merely tumble water around in
a circular motion. But water is in continual movement
through the seas. The water moves in currents, many of
which are invisible.

Some currents, for example the Gulf Stream of the Atlantic and its counterpart, the Kuroshio of the Pacific, flow
for thousands of miles through the oceans. The Kuroshio
(Japanese for "Black Stream") is so named because of its

A card enclosed in a drift bottle offers a reward for information about where and when the bottle was found. Sometimes drift bottles float across the Atlantic and are returned by European finders.

dark color. The Gulf Stream is deep blue. These and other great currents flow like rivers, that is, always in one direction. The Kuroshio and the Gulf Stream carry warm water from the tropics and flow northward, tempering the climate of the lands near which they pass. The Gulf Stream's effect is felt in Europe as well as along the east coast of North America, for water from the Gulf Stream continues across the ocean as the North Atlantic Current.

In addition to the riverlike currents, there are others of a different type created by the tide. The periodic increase and decrease in the depth of the sea caused by the tide is accompanied by a horizontal movement of water. These currents run in one direction for a certain number of hours when the tide is rising and in the reverse direction during the following period when the tide is falling. Some tidal currents flow so rapidly that the water swirls around in whirlpools.

Navigators need information about the direction and

speed of currents, for they can either help or hinder a ship's progress. If a ship travels against a current, it is slowed down; by traveling with a current a ship's speed is increased. The study of currents was undertaken for the purpose of aiding navigation, but it was soon realized that currents are not only important to seafarers but constitute a vast natural transportation system for sea water and everything in it: tiny fish and large ones, icebergs—even waste products.

Ever since the first men camped at the edge of the sea and traveled in boats, they have dumped waste into the water. Some waste sinks immediately, or almost immediately, to the ocean bottom. Other waste floats and is transported by currents. Scientists are concerned now about the spread of nuclear waste and other pollutants by currents. It is not yet known how long nuclear waste may remain afloat. A year after atomic bomb tests on islands in the Pacific, some fallout material was discovered in the North Equatorial Current, 3500 miles from the test site. Scientists have warned against disposing of atomic waste in the vicinity of the Gulf Stream because its channel is, in places, close to shore and waste carried by the Stream could contaminate coastal beaches.

The difficulties involved in tracking currents are so great that it is surprising how much has been discovered about them. One of the simplest and oldest ways of tracking ocean currents is with bottles. The recent experiment with the corked bottles—"drift bottles," scientists call them— was to find out about the currents flowing over the continental shelf of North America's east coast. (A continental shelf is the submerged part of a continent.) The direction in which drift bottles travel shows which way the current is moving; its speed is figured from the time required for bottles to be carried from one place to another. In the study of

the east-coast currents, the fastest movement of water was found to be in the vicinity of Cape Kennedy, Florida.

The scientists were not surprised that some of their bottles were found on European beaches, because in earlier experiments drift bottles had traveled across the Atlantic. The scientists assumed that, like other drift bottles, theirs had made the long voyage via the Gulf Stream and the North Atlantic Current.

Ships heading northward along the North American coast can get a real lift by traveling in the Gulf Stream. The problem is to locate the stream and stay in it, for its course and width continually change. Charts can only show the approximate course of the Stream.

The indispensable instrument for locating the boundaries of the Stream is a thermometer, since the water in the current is warmer than the temperature of the ocean on either side. Benjamin Franklin was the first to check on the location of the Gulf Stream with a thermometer. He made his tests while sailing to Europe on diplomatic missions and wisely concluded "that a thermometer may be a useful instrument for a navigator."

Since Franklin's time, inventors have developed many specialized kinds of thermometers for determining the temperature of the sea both at the surface and at lower levels. One kind is towed 650 feet below the sea's surface. At this level the water is unaffected by surface conditions. The thermometer continuously reports the water's temperature through a wire cable connected to a receiving instrument on the ship.

The deep-sea thermometer was originally intended for use by scientists, but its value as a navigational instrument has been proved by the captain of an oil tanker that operates between the Gulf of Mexico and Maine. On the trip to Maine the thermometer enables the captain to keep in the

center of the Gulf Stream, thus gaining maximum advantage from the north-flowing current. On the return trip to the Gulf of Mexico, the thermometer enables the captain to avoid the warm current, which would slow him down. By relying on the thermometer, the captain of the oil tanker has made speed records that none of his competitors has been able to equal.

Not only in temperature, but also in chemical composition, the water in the ocean's riverlike currents differs from the water through which it flows. One of the methods used by scientists to track such currents is chemical testing.

But neither a chemical nor a temperature test is of any value for tracking the currents near shore, caused by the rise and fall of the tide. Tidal currents do not move between banks of water of different temperature or chemical composition. Generally, all the water in a harbor or along a section of the coast moves in the tidal current.

Most tidal currents flow in one direction for about six hours and then, during the next six hours, in the reverse direction. The vertical movement of the tide is also reversed at intervals of about six hours. But the tide and the horizontal currents it causes frequently do not change at the same time. Odd though it may seem, tidal currents have an independent schedule. Some do not reverse their course until an hour or more after the tide has turned.

Another complication is that tidal currents may act differently in harbor A than in nearby harbor B. Therefore, each harbor must be separately studied.

The information that must be obtained includes the current's timing: that is, when the direction of its flow changes and the varying rate of speed at which the water runs. Tidal currents move slowly after they reverse course, and their speed gradually increases until they reach maximum velocity. Then the current slows down until the direction of its flow is again reversed.

Formerly, surveyors used a pole to determine the direction and speed of tidal currents. The pole, weighted at one end, floated vertically when cast into the water; the direction in which the pole was carried showed the current's course. Its speed was computed from the time required for a measured rope, attached near the top of the pole, to be pulled out. When handled by experts, current poles provide accurate information, but getting it is slow, hard work.

Today, automatic meters measure both the speed and direction of currents. One kind of meter contains a roll of 16 mm film on which measurements are recorded in code. Each time the water causes the meter's rotor to complete one revolution a dot is recorded on the film. Straight lines of varying lengths are recorded by the meter's compass mechanism to show the direction in which the water is flowing.

Another kind of current meter reports its measurements by radio. The transmitting equipment is in a float below

Radio current meters suspended below this float measure the speed and direction of currents. The measurements are transmitted to a receiver on the survey ship.

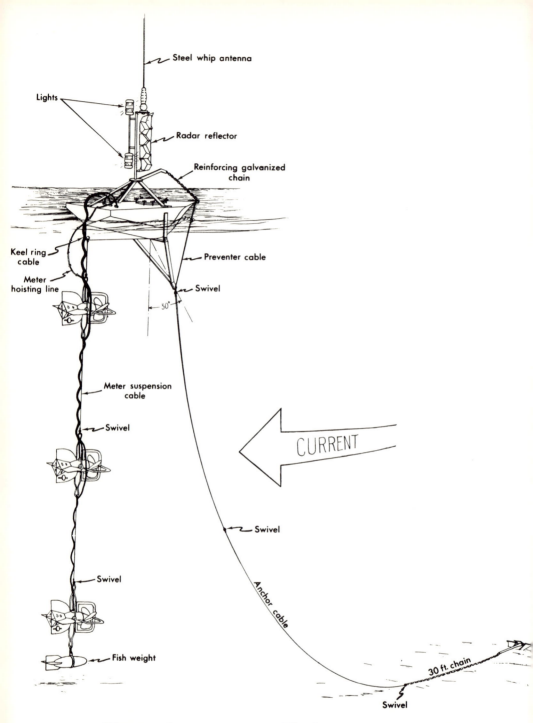

Steel whip antenna

Lights

Radar reflector

Reinforcing galvanized chain

Keel ring cable

Meter hoisting line

Preventer cable

Swivel

30°

Meter suspension cable

Swivel

CURRENT

Swivel

Swivel

Anchor cable

Fish weight

30 ft. chain

Swivel

Diagram of a current meter. The flowing current turns the propellers suspended below the meter, and the current velocity and direction are then transmitted to the survey ship.

which the meters are suspended. Two or more meters are hung below each float so that measurements of the current are obtained at different levels. Each meter has a propeller that is turned by the current, and the faster the current flows, the faster the propeller turns. At each revolution, it keys a signal. The meters hang on swivels and always face in the direction from which the current is flowing. The direction is reported by a second radio signal controlled by a compass within the meter. The two signals, one giving the current's velocity and the other its direction, are recorded on tape by a receiver on the survey ship.

Not only do the automatic meters report how currents move at the surface and at lower levels but, by anchoring groups of meters in a number of places, data can be collected for an area of many miles.

Tidal currents are also being traced by aerial photography. For a photographic survey of surface currents, a coloring material is usually put into the water. Finely ground aluminum flakes have been found to give excellent results. Paper bags containing a half pound of flakes were dropped from low-flying aircraft during a recent tidal current survey

Photographic record made by an automatic current meter. The broken black streaks show the direction of the current, and the dots indicate the speed at which it is flowing.

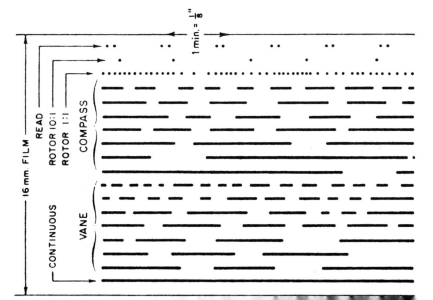

of Long Island Sound, a body of water approximately one hundred miles in length, partly in New York State and partly bordering Connecticut. At its eastern end the Sound is open to the Atlantic Ocean. When the tide rises, water from the Atlantic flows into the Sound and when the tide ebbs, water flows from the Sound to the ocean.

The flight plan for the photographic survey specified that the planes were to fly across the Sound on courses spaced two miles apart and drop a bag of flakes each half mile. When the bags hit the water and burst, the powder spreads out, making a silvery blotch. At one-hour intervals a plane flew over the Sound and photographed the blotches. The speed and direction of the current were determined from the changes in the positions of the silvery blotches from one set of pictures to the next.

Currents below the surface also were tracked photographically. For this part of the survey, floats were built of plywood and weighted plastic balls were attached to them on ropes 15 feet long. The floats were coated with fluorescent orange paint, which made them stand out on the color film and on the Sound itself. Even at night navigators could see the floats and avoid running them down. The balls suspended below each float moved with the current at the 15-foot level and pulled the float along. Thus the changing position of the floats shown on the aerial photograph provided the information needed for calculating the velocity and direction of the subsurface currents.

Since the surveying had to be discontinued during the blustery autumn and winter months, it took years before the required information was collected. After it was analyzed, a set of charts was prepared for the eastern part of Long Island Sound and its many bays, harbors, and rivers. One chart shows how the current acts at the moment that water from the ocean starts to flood into the Sound; a second

Tidal current charts show the direction and speed of currents for each hour of the day and tell navigators where current conditions are most favorable for them.

chart shows conditions one hour after the flood began; a third chart shows conditions two hours later; and so on. Altogether there are six charts covering the flood period. Arrows indicate the direction in which the water moves and numbers tell its speed.

Another group of hourly charts shows how the currents act during the period when their course is reversed and water from the Sound is ebbing back to the ocean. These charts supersede a set based on a survey made more than thirty years before.

There are many differences in the facts given by the new and old current charts due, probably, to the more accurate information obtained by modern surveying techniques.

Tidal current charts supply basic information that can be applied to any day of any year. However, to learn how currents will run on a specific day, navigators need both current charts and a book called *Tidal Current Tables.* This book, published annually by the National Ocean Survey, lists the predicted hour and minute that currents will change direction every day during the year at various parts of the coast.

Suppose a navigator wants to know how the current will affect him when he sails from the ocean into Long Island Sound at noon on July 4. He looks up July 4 in the tide tables and finds that the current will begin to flow into the Sound a little before 10 o'clock in the morning. In other words, the navigator will enter the Sound two hours after the current began to flow into it. He therefore turns to the current chart showing conditions two hours after the current began to flood into the Sound, sees where the current will be running most rapidly, and sets his course to take full advantage of the favorable current.

CHAPTER VIII

The Ice Patrol

The tracking of icebergs began after a terrible sea disaster. On the night of April 15, 1912, the passenger ship *Titanic* collided with an iceberg and sank. The casualty list of men, women, and children drowned totaled 1517. The great loss of life focused world-wide attention on the iceberg peril. Seamen had long been aware of it.

Icebergs from the Arctic arrive in the most heavily traveled parts of the North Atlantic during spring and early summer. This period is known as the iceberg season.

Although icebergs may be as long as a city street and tower hundreds of feet above the sea, they may not be visible until it is too late for a ship to swerve away. Captains need advance warning of where icebergs are lurking. Such warnings are broadcast twice daily by the International Ice Patrol.

After the sinking of the *Titantic,* the United States sent two Navy cruisers north, to patrol the shipping lanes during the remainder of the 1912 iceberg season. The next year the patrolling was done by the U. S. Coast Guard. The International Ice Patrol was created in 1914. At the Conference on the Safety of Life at Sea, thirteen nations voted to establish a patrol service and asked the United States to

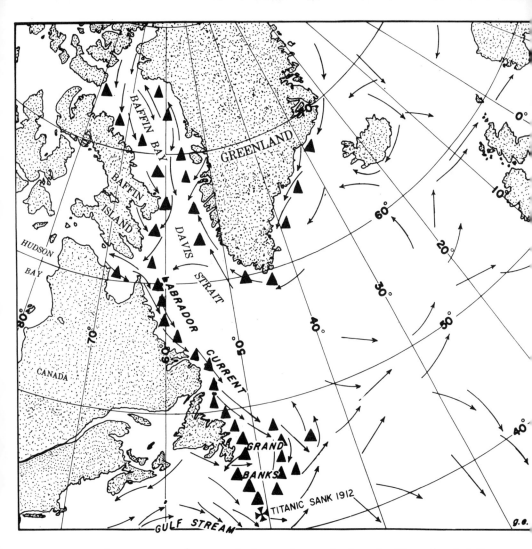

An average of 7,500 icebergs from glaciers in Greenland drift southward in the Labrador Current. About 400 bergs pass New-foundland each year.

operate it. All of the nations that signed the pact agreed to share the expenses. This system has satisfied the original members of the Ice Patrol and those who joined it later.

Responsibility for conducting the International Ice Patrol was entrusted to the U. S. Coast Guard. The patrolled area of more than 33,000 square miles is south of Newfoundland in the vicinity of the Grand Banks, a comparatively shallow part of the ocean.

The Banks are blanketed by fog much of the time. The fog, caused by the mingling of the water carried by two great ocean currents, the Labrador Current, which transports cold water from the Arctic, and the Gulf Stream, which transports warm water from the tropics, hides the icebergs that ride southward in the Labrador Current.

The shortest route for ships crossing the North Atlantic is close to the Grand Banks. The *Titanic* sank near the edge of the Banks. Now during the iceberg season, the Ice Patrol advises when ships should travel on a more southerly route in order to avoid areas of greatest danger. But even on a more southerly, and longer, route, icebergs may be encountered. Therefore the Ice Patrol's broadcasts giving the location of bergs are of prime importance. Every ship traveling in the North Atlantic tunes in the broadcasts.

During the first years of the Ice Patrol, the Coast Guard used ships to hunt bergs. Now most of the scouting is done by planes, and ships are used for special tasks, such as stand-

This 180-foot Coast Guard ship looks like a toy as she passes a gigantic iceberg near the Grand Banks. Ships are used for research in arctic seas.

ing guard near an especially dangerous berg. After the iceberg season, Coast Guard ships assigned to the Ice Patrol carry out oceanic research. When the Ice Patrol was established, one of its prescribed duties was to study the northern seas. This research has provided most of the facts we now know about the birth and life history of Arctic icebergs.

On one exciting expedition the ship *Northland,* commanded by "Iceberg" Smith, traveled up the west coast of Greenland to the glaciers that produce most of the icebergs carried to the Grand Banks by the Labrador Current. The *Northland* squeezed into fjords jammed with glittering bergs of gigantic sizes. Some, it was estimated, weighed a million and a half tons. The men saw and heard bergs being "calved." When a piece of a glacier breaks off and topples into the sea a new iceberg is born. It enters the water with a tremendous splash and a thunderous roar.

Ordinarily, the scientific exploration carried on by the Ice Patrol is less dramatic. One important, but unexciting, task is recording the temperature of the water at, and below, the surface and collecting samples of the water to determine its chemical composition. The course, speed, and boundaries of the Labrador Current are being established by these tests.

Information about the current enables experts to estimate where a berg drifting today will be tomorrow. The ability to make such estimates is of tremendous importance because there are frequent periods during the iceberg season when the fog is so dense that scouting flights cannot be made.

The distance from the iceberg-producing glaciers on the West Greenland coast to the Grand Banks is about 3000 miles. An iceberg can make this long voyage in about eleven months. Fortunately, only a small percentage of those that start southward complete the trip. Some are trapped in bays along the route, others drift into shallow spots in the ocean and are stranded there. The part of a

berg visible above water is only about one-fifth of the total ice mass; the rest is submerged. Large bergs may extend 600 feet below the sea's surface. There are many places in the vicinity of the Grand Banks where the water is not deep enough for such a berg to remain afloat. It digs into the sea bottom and is held fast until the ice melts or breaks.

Because the greater part of an iceberg is under water, its movement is controlled chiefly by currents. But wind also propels bergs. When experts estimate how rapidly ice will drift, and in what direction, wind conditions are always taken into account.

Months before icebergs reach the North Atlantic shipping lanes, Ice Patrol planes make reconnaissance flights along the coasts of Newfoundland, Labrador, and Baffin Island. The number and location of bergs sighted indicates whether the coming iceberg season will be unusually dangerous or average. If, during these pre-season flights, about 1500 bergs are counted, the season will be average. About 300 of the bergs will float down to the Grand Banks area.

The observer on an Ice Patrol plane needs sharp eyes and special training to spot and estimate the size of icebergs.

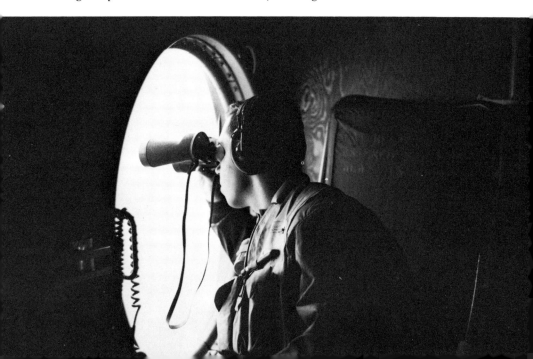

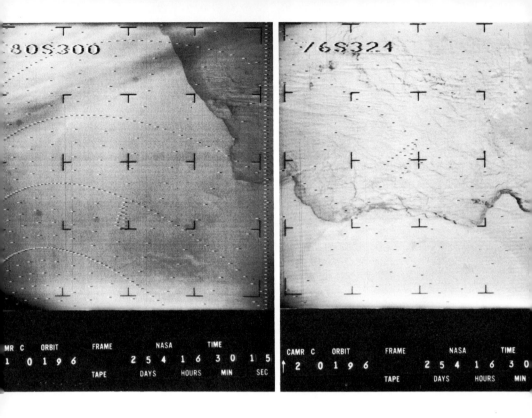

The location of bergs sighted during pre-season flights is plotted on a large map kept at the Ice Patrol's Headquarters in the Coast Guard Base on Governors Island, New York. Concentration of ten or more icebergs are indicated on the map by a + sign and one, or a few bergs, by a dot. The appearance of a berg may be so distinctive that it can be recognized when sighted on later flights. It may have twin peaks or the ice may be scooped out at the water line so that the berg resembles an island with a large bay. Generally, however, the appearance of bergs changes rapidly. Large bergs may split into a number of smaller ones or a berg may capsize, with the result that its appearance is entirely changed.

The newest source of information about icebergs is pictures taken by satellites. The polar orbiting satellites that move over remote parts of the Arctic and Antarctic have

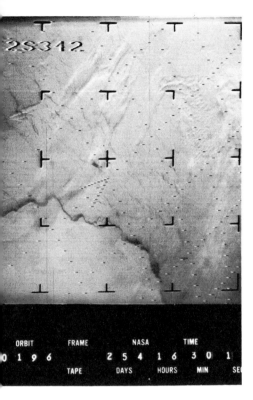

Three photographs of the ice-encrusted coast of the Weddell Sea in the Antarctic taken by the satellite Nimbus II. Such pictures are invaluable for mapping purposes. Satellite pictures also show the movement of icebergs.

made many pictures of great value. The satellite known as Nimbus II made a series of pictures of the ice-encrusted coastline of the Weddell Sea in the Antarctic that were useful for mapping purposes. Nimbus II also took pictures, during a six-week period, of an iceberg drifting southward along the Greenland coast.

If identifying marks could be placed on icebergs, tracking them would be easier. Experiments have been made in shooting dyes on bergs. Arrows tipped with dye-filled glass capsules were shot at icebergs from the deck of a research ship. When the arrows hit the ice, the capsules broke and the dye made a big stain. Red, green, and four shades of blue dye were used.The project was discontinued because the stains lasted only a few days.

During the iceberg season ships sailing the North Atlantic supply information about weather and ice conditions to

Chart of Rongelap Atoll in the Pacific printed over a photograph of the area taken by Gemini V astronauts shows the usefulness of spacecraft pictures for mapping.

the Ice Patrol. The reports include the location of all ice sighted: big bergs, small ones called "growlers," and cakes of sea ice. The reports also give the strength and direction of the wind that the ships are encountering, the temperature of the sea and air, and the extent of visibility.

When the sighting of ice is reported, the Ice Patrol broadcasts the news and sends out a search plane as soon as possible. The weather information supplied by ships aids the Ice Patrol in planning its flight schedules. Planes are not sent to an area reported to be blanketed by fog or whipped by high winds. Perfect flying weather is rare in the Ice Patrol's territory, but conditions must be good enough for the flyers to do their hunting.

A flight plan is worked out before a plane takes off from the Canadian airfield where it is based. The plan specifies

the area to be searched and the lines on which the plane is to fly over it. When visibility is good, the planned flight lines may be 50 miles apart; on other days the lines may be no more than 25 miles apart. The lookouts on the planes must be able to see halfway from one flight line to another.

Ice Patrol planes fly low, often at less than half a mile above the sea, and they fly relatively slowly. If the planes were to fly at their full speed they might whiz by bergs before they could be seen.

Some bergs are detected by radar. A berg reflects back the radio signal transmitted by the plane's radar set and appears as a blob on its picture screen. The plane then swoops down so that a visual inspection can be made. Radar is far more effective for detecting icebergs when used from a plane than from a ship. Even a big berg may not show on a ship's radar screen until it is too late for the ship to avoid running into the ice.

The lookout on an Ice Patrol plane estimates the size of the berg sighted; the navigator usually determines the location of the ice by the electronic navigational system called "loran" (*lo*ng *ra*nge *na*vigation). Loran is used today by almost all large ships and airplanes to determine their position when far from shore.

Special radio receivers and charts are needed for loran navigation. The receiver is first tuned to the frequency on which one pair of loran stations broadcasts. The stations, one called "the master," the other "the slave," transmit signals consisting of short pulses. The time interval between the reception of the signals from the two stations is clocked by the loran receiver. The navigator then can identify one particular line on his loran chart on which he is located. But he still does not know his position on the line. To find that exact point, the navigator tunes in another pair of loran stations and from their signals identifies a second line on which

he is located. The plane is at the spot where the two lines cross on the chart. Determining a position by loran takes only a few minutes.

During the first years of the Ice Patrol, navigators of Coast Guard ships were obliged, when operating in fog, to rely on the method called "dead reckoning" to determine the ship's position and also that of bergs. Dead reckoning means figuring out where a ship is located by her speed and by the time and direction she has been traveling from a known position. Thus, if a ship has been traveling for ten hours at ten knots (nautical miles per hour) on a northerly course, she is located, by dead reckoning, one hundred nautical miles north of the location at which the navigator started his reckoning. But the wind or current may have decreased or increased the vessel's speed, or a cross wind may have pushed the ship to one or the other side of the projected course. Dead reckoning is not an exact system, and errors are unavoidable when it is used for determining the position of icebergs or ships. The mapping done by loran-equipped planes and ships is far more accurate.

When a patrol plane returns from a flight, the maps that the flyers have made of ice they have sighted, and the flyers' notes about the size and shape of bergs, are immediately transmitted by teletype to the experts at the Ice Patrol headquarters in New York. Their charts are promptly updated to show the location of all known icebergs, and a new, or revised, warning bulletin is prepared for broadcast to ships.

Hunting icebergs and giving prompt information about them to mariners is still the only way to protect ships from the silent white killers. No method has yet been found to destroy bergs. The Ice Patrol has unsuccessfully tried to shatter them with dynamite and gunfire. But the bergs float on until they drift out of the cold Labrador Current and melt in the warmer water carried north by the Gulf Stream.

This head-on picture of an Ice Patrol plane was taken on a clear day. On many days during the iceberg season fog makes such flights impossible.

CHAPTER IX

Why Pilot Charts Are

Given Away

Every month thousands of charts of a special kind are sent free of charge by the United States Naval Oceanographic Office to seafarers of all nations. These Pilot Charts, as they are called, show, for the month they cover, in what direction, and how hard, the wind generally blows in different parts of the North Atlantic and Pacific Oceans, the speed and course of ocean currents, where fog is likely to be encountered, and other facts about weather and sea conditions.

Since the first Pilot Charts were issued more than a hundred years ago, they have been given to mariners in return for assistance in providing the government's chart makers with information. Matthew Fontaine Maury initiated this system. It was his idea to chart the oceans' winds and currents. To carry out this vast project, he needed the co-operation of seafarers. Their help is still required.

Maury conceived his novel charting idea long before he was in a position to carry it out. While serving on Navy ships he concluded that winds and currents make natural paths through the seas and that if these paths were known,

ocean travel would be safer and faster. The question was how to track the natural paths. Maury found the answer after he had been crippled in a stagecoach accident and could no longer sail the seas.

In 1842, Maury was appointed head of the Navy's Depot of Charts and Instruments, a job that he made scientifically important. When Maury started work at the Depot, the Navy had few charts; navigators of warships sailing to and from Washington through Chesapeake Bay used charts made by the British before the American Revolution.

While searching through the Depot's storeroom, Maury made a valuable find: a collection of handwritten records of ocean voyages that Navy ships had made. Each of the dusty logbooks told the port from which the ship had started her voyage, the date, the routes sailed, when and where the ship had made fast time with favorable winds, or had been delayed by head winds and adverse currents. Maury grew more and more excited as he scanned the pages of the logbooks. Here was material with which he could begin charting winds and currents.

First Maury made separate piles of the books according to the voyages that they described. Thus, all records of voyages to Rio de Janeiro, Brazil, were put into one pile, those of voyages to the Gulf of Mexico were put into another pile, and so on. Then Maury listed the direction and force of the winds and currents reported by each ship that had sailed to the same destination. Maury dated each item on his list. After he had analyzed a number of logbooks, Maury could tell, for the areas included, the general wind patterns and the prevailing set of the ocean currents for different seasons of the year.

The accuracy of any statement as to average conditions depends to a large degree on the number of records on which it is based. Twenty-four records of voyages to Rio

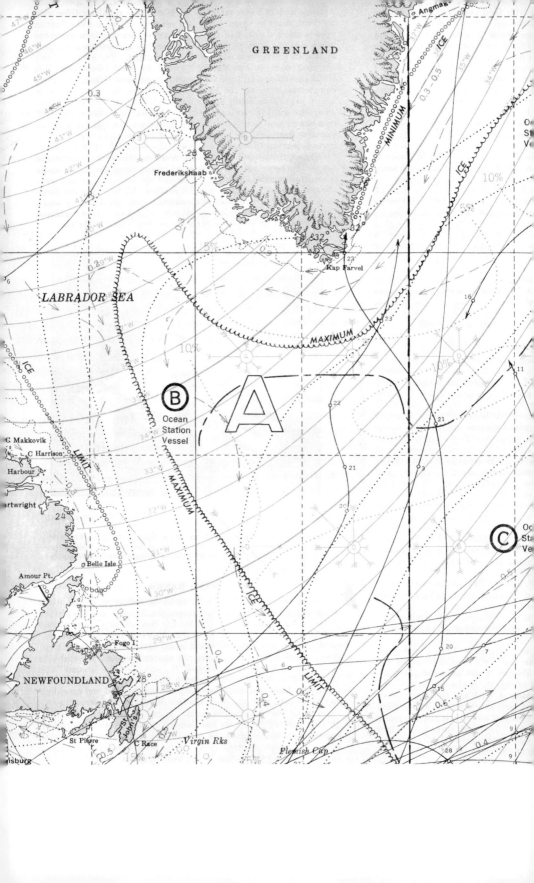

Section of a recent Pilot Chart of the North Atlantic. This chart shows conditions during the month of March. The arrows show the direction of currents and the figures tell their speed.

Photograph of Matthew Fontaine Maury at the height of his scientific career, when he was planning for international co-operation in meteorology.

will give a more accurate picture of average conditions than twelve records. Maury knew that he needed more data, and after working for some months on the old logbooks, he presented his plan for wind and current charts to his chief and asked that he direct skippers of Navy ships to provide additional information. Captains of commercial ships were also requested to send in data, but few did. Answering Maury's questions meant extra work. Mariners had not yet learned that each one of them would benefit by supplying information for the new kind of chart.

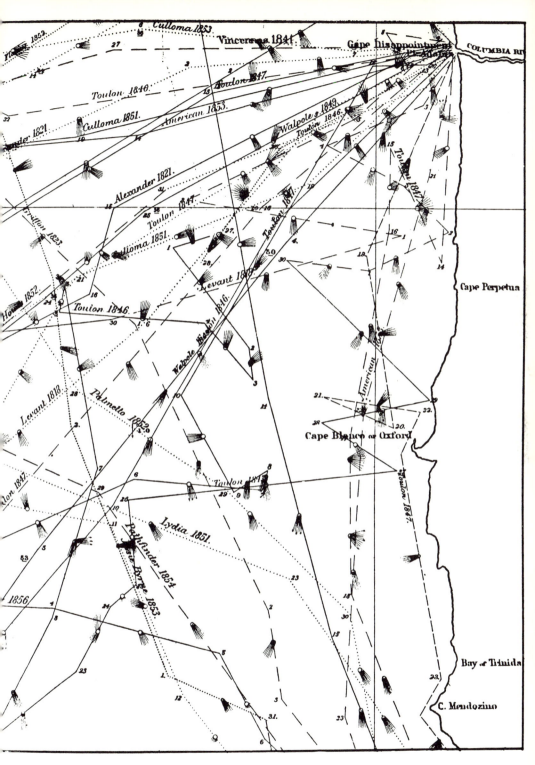

Section of one of Maury's first charts of the North Pacific used by ships carrying gold miners to California. The brushes show the direction of the wind. The ships that supplied information are named on the chart with the dates of their voyages.

Painting of the frigate Potomac in Valparaiso harbor, Chile. Maury sailed back to the United States in the Potomac after the voyage during which he conceived the idea of charting winds and currents.

The lack of co-operation did not stop Maury. He continued to cull facts from the old logbooks and to supplement them with whatever new information he received. In 1847, five years after he began work on his novel project, the first wind and current chart was published. It showed conditions in the Gulf of Mexico.

Maury was acquainted with John Quincy Adams, who was then a member of Congress, and he sent him a copy of the chart together with a letter in which he wrote:

"You will observe, by this chart, that the general currents

in the Gulf of Mexico are almost as regular in their courses and as sharp in their outlines as is the Mississippi River itself. So that, with this sheet as a guide, a vessel, by turning a little to the right, or a little to the left, according to its indications, may convert an unfavorable into a favorable current and the reverse."

Maury went on to say that seven charts of the Atlantic would soon be issued. He was especially enthusiastic about his directions for voyages to Rio de Janeiro. Years before, when Maury was sailing master of a sloop of war bound for Rio, he had searched unsuccessfully for such directions.

However, for a long time captains paid no attention to Maury's directions. They continued to sail their old routes on which they had to battle head winds and adverse currents. Finally the captain of a ship named *Wright* sailed as Maury recommended and made record-breaking time. The *Wright* sailed from Virginia to Rio in 38 days and returned in 37 days—the round trip was completed in about the same length of time ships ordinarily required just to reach Rio.

Word of this feat spread from captain to captain and from port to port. In a very short time Maury received many requests for the new wind and current charts and for his detailed sailing directions. Ship owners and captains wanted them because fast voyages increase profits. But the charts and directions were not for sale. Captains could obtain them only by agreeing to record their observations and send them to Maury.

Before long he had more than a thousand volunteer observers and was able to construct wind and current charts of the Pacific as well as of the Atlantic. Now Pilot Charts for the most traveled parts of the oceans are issued monthly, and charts of other areas are published in atlases that are revised from time to time. The information given on Pilot

Microscopic shells dredged from the sea bottom in mid-Atlantic convinced Maury that a submerged telegraph cable between Europe and America would not be destroyed by currents.

Charts is based on observations made over a period of many years. Some may date back to Maury's times.

Today, mariners who travel in the less frequented parts of the oceans are asked to supply sketches or photographs of coasts and harbors. Also, copies of the records made by the ship's echo-sounding equipment (fathograms) are requested. The need for the sounding records is emphasized in the technical manual supplied to marine observers. It says: "It is only through the co-operation and efforts of all ships that the vital task of charting the ocean floor can be completed. The task is too gigantic for survey vessels alone to accomplish."

Reports from observers are used not only for Pilot Charts but also for keeping other charts and navigational publications accurate and up to date. Observers are asked to report everything that they themselves would be interested in hearing about. Report to us, the government's chart makers say, and we will report to the maritime world. Observers send in most of their reports by mail, but they are instructed to report by radio telephone anything about which navigators

The building with the dome is the naval observatory in which Lieutenant Maury carried out his scientific work. He lived in the square building to the left.

need immediate warning. The government pays the charges for the call. Anything adrift on the sea—ice, a wreck, even a big log—that could damage a ship's hull or propellers is reported by telephone.

Sometimes telephoned reports, like the one made by the captain of the steamer *Bright Star*, are about a dramatic event. The captain reported that an undersea volcano near the Philippine Islands was erupting. The news was relayed to the Navy's office in Honolulu, which immediately broadcast a warning of the danger. Later, Navy ships and planes were sent to the area of the eruption to determine what changes the volcano had caused. As soon as the facts were gathered, mariners were informed of the changes to be made on their charts.

The captain of the *Bright Star* supplemented his telephoned report with a written one in which he supplied details about the eruption he had witnessed. The two reports were used as the basis for an article on undersea volcanoes that was printed on the back of a Pilot Chart. Articles about the sea are frequently published on the back of

monthly Pilot Charts. For this reason many navigators keep their copies of these charts for a long time. Even though the information on the chart itself is outdated, the technical article printed on the back is interesting and valuable.

Copies of Pilot Charts are sent only to people who continue to serve the chart makers. Once each year the government reviews its mailing list and eliminates the names of observers who have failed to co-operate. If a man has not made a single report during the previous twelve months, he loses the privilege of receiving Pilot Charts free of charge. These charts are available to students and others interested in studying the ocean and can be obtained at a very modest cost from government agencies that sell nautical charts.

CHAPTER X

Keeping Charts

Up to Date

"Stop the presses!" The order was given only a short time after the printing of a new navigational chart had been started.

Surveyors had worked for months making measurements and recording information for the new chart. The experts who compiled the chart had studied hundreds of records and aerial photographs. After the chart was completed, it was checked and rechecked many times before being approved for printing. Yet, despite all the care that had been taken, a change had to be made.

The reason for the sudden stop order was the receipt, by the chief of the chart division, of a radioed message giving important new information about one area included in the chart.

This was not the first time a correction was required while a chart was being printed, nor will it be the last. For information that was correct yesterday may be incorrect today because of natural changes or new findings. A major problem with which chart makers must cope is keeping their products up to date.

Charts are printed by the process known as photolithography. First the chart manuscript (the original drawing of the chart) is photographed. Enormous cameras are used; some weigh close to 15 tons and are capable of making negatives as large as 45 inches by 65 inches. Any imperfections in a negative are eliminated by engravers skilled in this type of hand work. Then aluminum plates for the printing are made from the negative. Photolithography is a very satisfactory method for producing charts because the printing plates are comparatively inexpensive. Another advantage is the speed and accuracy with which colors can be reproduced. A number of different colors are used on charts to make them easier to read and to emphasize various features. Thus, blue is used for shallow water near shore, buff for land areas, green for marshes and exposed ledges, and purplish red (magenta) for the lines indicating anchorage areas. Some charts are printed in as many as seven colors. Multicolor, high-speed lithographic offset presses produce thousands of such charts an hour.

The temperature and humidity of a chart printing plant is most carefully controlled. The purpose of the air conditioning is not to make the plant comfortable for the workers but to safeguard the storage of chart paper. Dry air causes paper to shrink and humid air causes paper to stretch. Even the slightest change in the dimensions of the paper used for charts must be prevented. If this were not done, all the care taken to determine, and to show, the exact position on a chart of navigational markers or of rocks and other dangers would be wasted.

The printing of a chart does not end the work that must be done on it by the government experts. Frequently, they must correct charts. If, for instance, a new navigational marker has been set out by the Coast Guard, the position of the marker must be shown on all charts of the area before

Imperfections in the negative of a chart are corrected by engravers skilled in this type of work. Absolute accuracy is required.

they are sold. Or, if a ship sinks, the location of the new wreck must be indicated. Until 1968, when a "screen printing press" was put into service to aid in correcting charts, all changes were made by hand. Can you imagine the amount of work involved in hand-correcting five million charts? That was the workload in one typical year at the Naval Oceanographic Office. The new press can correct three hundred charts in about twenty minutes. Changes are printed in green ink. Each chart sold is stamped with the date to which it has been corrected.

After a chart has been purchased, it is up to the navigator to mark changes on it. The corrections to be made are published in a weekly government bulletin called "Notices to Mariners." Although the average price of a chart is less than two dollars, it is neither necessary nor practical to purchase a new chart when minor corrections are required. A large ship may carry hundreds of charts, and buying new ones for each reported change during a year would add up to a considerable sum. Chart maintenance is a tedious job, but on both government and commercial ships it is one of the routine tasks for which the navigational department is responsible. Usually the work is assigned to a junior officer.

The Naval Oceanographic Office lists more than 6000 charts of the world's oceans, coasts, and ports, and prints ten million copies of them annually. The National Ocean Survey's list includes about 800 charts of the coastal waters of the United States and its possessions, and prints more than two million copies of these charts each year. Of course, the demand for some charts is greater than for others, and before deciding how many copies of any chart to print, estimates are made of the number that will be sold in a year or two. The supply on hand is checked periodically, and as the stock of a chart dwindles, the charting authorities decide whether to reprint it, to issue a new edition, or to prepare an entirely new chart. If no important changes have occurred in the area covered by the chart, it is reprinted from the same plates used for the previous printing. But if there have been many changes, the negatives are revised and a new edition is printed. About 80 new editions and 20 entirely new charts are published annually by the National Ocean Survey. Obsolete charts that the government has in stock are destroyed. Navigators likewise discard their old charts; navigating with an out-of-date chart is dangerous.

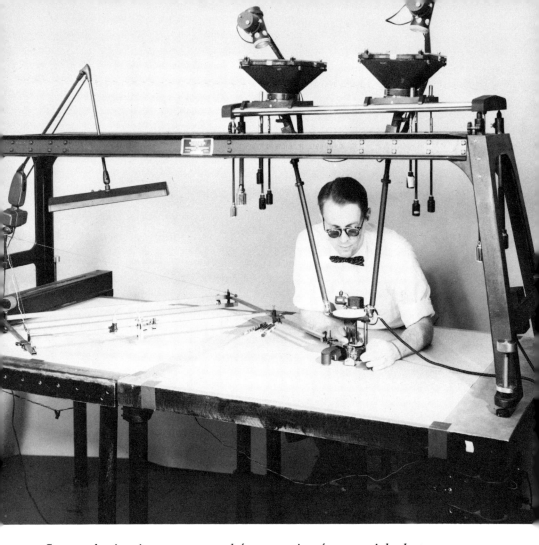

Stereo-plotting instrument used for mapping from aerial photographs. The map maker, by getting a three-dimensional perspective, can determine exact locations and heights.

The original drawings made during a survey are stored in a fireproof vault and are examined when either a new edition or a new chart is being prepared. Among the other records checked is one called a "History." It is a complete list of all the data used or consulted when the chart was originally prepared. So much material is kept for each chart that a way had to be found to solve the storage problem. The solution was photographing the records on microfilm. The small rolls of film are easy to store, and the prints made of the films add a safety feature. Films and prints are stored in separate locations, sometimes many miles apart, so that if either is damaged or destroyed during some disaster, the other would preserve the records.

In the years ahead, many new devices will undoubtedly be developed for charting the oceans. One may be a robot-controlled boat to carry out survey operations. But not even the smartest electronic robots will ever eliminate the need for human experts to explore and chart the oceans.

Index

103

oceans and determining composition of the sea bottom.
Maps:
  and charts of Mercator, 20-22, 25-28, 30
  and records of Columbus's four voyages to America, as guarded state secrets, 7
  of the sea, official, issued by 15th-century Spain, 9
  see also Chart; Charting; Charts
Markers, anchored (buoys), 31
Maury, Matthew Fontaine, pioneer in charting the seas, 49
  initiator of Pilot Charts, 86, 87, 89, 90
  letter from, to John Quincy Adams, 92-93
  photograph of, 90
  wind and current charts compiled by, 86-93
Maury, Navy survey ship, survey expedition of, 49-55
  echo sounders, as part of equipment of, 49-50, 52
Measuring devices, old and modern, used by surveyors in mapping and measuring, 35, 36, 38
Mediterranean Sea, Portolan chart of, 29
Mercator charts (and maps), 20-22, 25-28, 30
  compass roses printed on charts, 28
  to find direction, and great-circle chart, to determine shortest route, 26, 27
  unit for measuring distance on, 30
Mercator, Gerardus, Flemish map maker and designer of framework used for most sea charts and land maps, 20-22, 25-28, 30
Minutes, as measurements of latitude and longitude, 22
  unit for measuring distance in minutes of latitude, 30, 31
Mountains, submerged, detected and charted by echo sounders, 15

National Ocean Survey:
  navigational booklet, Chart No. I, 31, 32
  publishers of charts of U.S. coastal waters, 9, 28, 41
  wreck-hunting expeditions of, 57
  see also Hassler, Ferdinand R.: Pilot Charts
Naval Oceanographic Office, charts of, 9, 45, 99, 100
Navigation, safe, information for, as provided by scientific mapping and charting, 5

Navigational chart, information supplied by, 30
  abbreviations and code symbols used on, 31
  see also Pilot Charts
Navigational system, electronic ("loran"), 83, 84
Navy's Depot of Charts and Instruments,
  Maury appointed head of, 87
Nimbus II, satellite pictures made by, of ice-encrusted coast of the Weddell Sea, 81
North and South Poles, and circles of latitude, 23
North Atlantic Current, 65, 67
North Equatorial Current, fallout material discovered in, 66
North latitude, degrees of, as numbered and measured from the equator to the Poles, 22, 23
North, or zero, line on compass rose, 28
"Notices to Mariners," government bulletin, 100
Nuclear waste and other pollutants, transported by ocean currents, 66

Obstructions in the water, methods of locating, 58-62
Ocean bottom, graph of, using echo sounder on survey vessel, 14, 15, 16-17 (chart)
Ocean currents, tracking the, 64-74
Oceans:
  charting the, as one of biggest and most challenging mapping projects, 5
  depth of ocean water, methods of measuring, 12-20
Oceans' winds and currents, charting of, 86-93

Pacific Ocean canyon, 18
Philippine Islands, charting of Luzon Island's jungles and coastal waters, by U.S. Navy surveyors, 45-49
Photography, aerial, surveyors' use of, to determine depth of water, 43-45, 101
Photolithography, process used for producing charts, 98-99
"Phyllis" (typhoon), 53
Pilot Charts, 86-89, 93-96
Pilot Major, Spanish official responsible for making additions and corrections to his government's master set of charts, 8
Planes used by Ice Patrol, to hunt icebergs, 77, 79, 80, 82-85

106

107

Thermometer, for locating boundaries of Gulf Stream, 67
Tidal currents, direction, speed, and independent schedule of, 68, 69, 73, 74
Tidal Current Tables, 74
Tide gauge, 54, 55
Titanic, sinking of, after collision with iceberg, 75, 77
Transmitters and radio signals, surveyors' use of, 42
Treasure hunt, and sunken British warships, 57
Triangles and triangulation, method of accurate mapping, 36, 37, 40
Typhoon "Phyllis," 53

Undersea oil wells in Gulf of Mexico, 60, 61
Undersea volcano near Philippine Islands, report of, by Captain of the *Bright Star,* 95
Underwater treasure hunt, and sunken British warships, 57
Underwater volcanic seamount, graph of, 15
U.S. Coast Guard:
    as ice patrol in shipping lanes, 75-78, 84
    planes used by, 77, 79, 80, 82, 83
    ships used by, 77, 78
        see also Satellite pictures, as

source of information about icebergs, 80, 81
U.S. Congress, authorization by, for charting coastal waters of the United States, 33, 37
U.S. Naval Oceanographic Office, 30, 45
    Pilot Charts issued by, 86-89, 93-96

Volcanic seamount, underwater, graph of, 15

Waste and other pollutants, transported by ocean currents, 66
Weddell Sea, ice-encrusted coast of, in the Antarctic, satellite pictures of, 81
West and East longitude explained, 24
Wind and current charts, 86-93
Wire-drag survey technique, for complete search of sea bottom, 20, 58-62
Wreck-hunting expeditions, 57-63
"Wrecking crews" (government experts),
    duties of, 58, 60
Wright, record-breaking time of ship's round trip, from Virginia to Rio, using Maury's chart, 93

Zero, or north, line on compass rose, 28

Samples of the water at different depths are obtained by lowering a number of open metal cylinders fastened to a wire cable. A "messenger" slides down the cable and when it strikes a container it turns over and closes, sealing in a sample of water. Its temperature is automatically recorded. After the cylinders are pulled up, chemical tests are made of the water.

SCUBA divers go down to make first hand observations on the bottom.

Geological dredges are used to collect samples of the rocks on the sea bottom. Vast deposits of manganese, a mineral required in the manufacture of steel, have been discovered by dredging operations.

Stereocameras with powerful lights are lowered to photograph the sea bottom.